ADRIAEN BROUWER

ADRIAEN BROUWER

TRANSLATED FROM THE DUTCH TEXT BY
J. G. TALMA-SCHILTHUIS AND ROBERT WHEATON

Gerhardus

GERARD KNUTTEL

ADRIAEN BROUWER

THE MASTER AND HIS WORK

L. J. C. BOUCHER · THE HAGUE

MDCCCCLXII

PREFACE

Adriaen Brouwer, in the words of Wilhelm von Bode, was 'ein Meister der unter allen Nieder-ländischen Meistern des XVII Jahrhunderts nächst Rembrandt und Rubens der genialste ist.'

This considered judgement by so able a critic deserves to be endorsed here. Yet the studies that Bode has devoted to the master testify to the fallibility of even one of the greatest German scholars of Netherlands Art History. The work of another authority in this field, Dr. F. Schmidt Degener, is also faulty; its author always hoped, in fact, that he would be able to correct in a later publication his early work on Brouwer—which he called his 'youthful indiscretion'. This book was published in 1908; Bode's monograph appeared in 1924. Today the general opinion is that many conclusions reached in these studies are no longer acceptable.

Although a few detail-studies on Brouwer have appeared since 1924 (see the Bibliography at the end of the book), giving a clearer insight into some facets, no new comprehensive picture of the master and his work has been undertaken.

Since Bode's monograph not a single new fact or datum has become known which might throw additional light on the life of the artist, or afford a novel insight into his work. More-over, only a few paintings have appeared which were not already known to Bode. Working with the already known historical facts and works of art, my task has been this: to produce a new critical evaluation, ordering and sifting of the œuvre; and on this basis to construct a new picture of the master's life and personality, and of his artistic development.

Unlike my illustrious predecessors I had the advantage of access to an almost complete, excellently arranged collection of study material in the Rijksbureau voor Kunsthistorische Documentatie in The Hague. Without this material and the generous cooperation of the staff of the Bureau, I could not have worked to construct an image which I hope is worthy to be considered along with—or rather opposite to—the conception presented by Schmidt Degener and Bode.

By the time of his early death Brouwer had already achieved celebrity as an artist, and no less as an habitué of taverns and a debtor. The earliest biographers devote themselves all too eagerly to romanticizing this extremely picturesque figure on the fringes of society. In this way an overgrowth of anecdotes and gossip obscured the image of the creative artist. The reliable archival facts are extremely few. Since he signed not one work with his full name, there are only a few works which can be accepted with complete confidence to serve as a beginning

5

point for the reconstruction of his œuvre. This reconstruction required the application of a very high standard: the few trustworthy works testify to an unmatched technical mastery and a rarely reached artistic height, steadily maintained.

Not this level of achievement, however, but the subject matter soon came to be accepted as the characteristic of a Brouwer. Copies in the graphic arts were provided with his name if the original was at all like Brouwer—and he had many imitators. 'Brouwer' became a concept defined by certain motifs and not by artistic quality. To purify his œuvre it was necessary to apply a standard if anything too high, rather than too lax; for the indulgent spirit of Bode's book is by far its greatest flaw.

His purportedly dissipated way of life does not appear to have influenced his intense powers of concentration as a painter; consequently we may at least cast doubt on the accuracy of these tales of depravity.

Many colleagues, collectors, museum directors and art dealers, both in the Netherlands and elsewhere, have contributed in the most sympathetic manner to the realization of this study— and have made my work a pleasure.

I wish to mention particularly the Rijksbureau voor Kunsthistorische Documentatie in The Hague, the Witt Library in London, and the staffs of the Louvre, the Berlin-Dahlem Museum and the Metropolitan Museum in New York. In the storage depots of these museums I was able to study works not on display, which had been rightly or wrongly ascribed to Brouwer. When the Berlin collection was temporarily removed to Wiesbaden, I enjoyed the same privilege through the kindness of the director, Prof. Dr. Ernst Holzinger.

To all these go my hearty thanks. I would, moreover, have been at a loss without the continuous help of my assistant, Mrs. A. Callenbach-van Aken, during the six years that I was occupied with this book and her successor Mrs. M. L. Jonkers-Reineke.

The translators, Mrs. J. G. Talma-Schilthuis and Robert Wheaton, deserve acknowledgment and praise for having gone to more trouble than was required simply to produce an accurate English translation of my Dutch text.

The Hague, September, 1961   GERARD KNUTTEL

PART I

1. Ant. van Dyck, Portrait of Adriaen Brouwer

Coll. Duke of Buccleuch

PERSONALITY AND LIFE

Who was Adriaen Brouwer? A great artist—and yet a besotted rake, a buffoon and an habitual debtor, who died of loose living in January 1638 at the age of thirty-two... or so his biographers would have us believe. His portraits present us with an elegant gentleman; yet he does not appear to have sought out refined society. He must have been a man of intellectual culture, since he was taken into the Haarlem and Antwerp 'Rederijkerskamers',—rhetoricians' clubs.[1] His property was small and he did not have many books—but more than most artists of his time. If he preferred to paint life against a shabby background, he did it in the most sensitive and careful manner.

Arnold Houbraken's motley, fascinating biography, in his 'Groote Schouburgh der Nederlantsche Konstschilders en Schilderessen', portrays him as pre-eminently the dandified rake and practical joker.[2] It appeared in 1718, eighty years after Brouwer's death, and has become the more or less definite biography. Houbraken's narrative drew on rumours and stories then current, and on the older biographies of Cornelis de Bie (1662), Joachim von Sandrart (1675), and Isaac Bullart (published in 1682, but written earlier). These writings show how strongly the short life of this bohemian genius appealed to the imagination of his contemporaries and of those who lived shortly after. No one seems to have doubted the fact of his genius. Houbraken's biography, however, shows little evidence of what we today regard as the essential values of Brouwer's art. Wherein, one wonders, lies the greatness of the master, which the author emphatically asserts...

His work illustrates the paradox of his life: coarse scenes in low taverns, fights among card players and tipplers, men dulled by the narcotic effects of tobacco, while a pig laps up the drunkard's vomit—all lovingly painted with the tip of the brush, with the greatest tenderness of tonality and colour gradation, with textures sensitively rendered, with sparkling pinpoints of light, with the subtlety of a flower-painter—yet without detracting from the force and harshness of the picture. It appears from the early biographies that people used to see only

[1] 'Rederijkerskamers' in this period were societies whose members cultivated eloquence and poetry, and performed plays.

[2] Houbraken writes à propos of one of his jokes: 'Nor was he wanting in intelligence. Often his jokes were a cloak for his cleverness. For this reason we show a monkey beside his portrait in Plate O.' (This portrait, an etching, is a copy of the well-known print by Schelte à Bolswert after van Dyck.) Houbraken apparently thought he could best characterize the great master with a monkey for an attribute.

drollery in these scenes, rather than acute, psychologically penetrating portrayals of the out-
casts of society. Brouwer, in a spirit of psychological 'naturalism' (in the nineteenth century
sense of the word), laid bare passions and frailties without the idealizing or compassion of
Ostade, in Holland, or of Teniers, in Flanders, and entirely without the moralizing or emblem-
atizing of van de Venne. The pathos of these insights escaped the biographers; but Rubens,
and particularly Rembrandt, must have looked deeper, since they tried so hard to acquire his
rare paintings. These were hardly the painters to pay such a high price for an anecdotal
canvas. And technical merit was prized by art-lovers as well as creative artists in the seventeenth century. Artistic susceptibility is not solely the prerogative of creative artists; it may
be no less present in the sensitive art-lover, incapable though he is of original creation.

Brouwer could sell his work easily, but he insisted on a good price; he would have preferred
burning it to accepting too low a price. Why then was he always in debt? Perhaps because of
his free and easy attitude toward property, reported in an epitaph, probably made up by
de Bie:

> 'He never despised what the world on him pressed:
> He painted but slowly, could spend like the best,
> And in low piss-pot taverns smoke his pipe with a zest.'

What is remarkable is the phrase: 'He painted but slowly.' This was a consequence not so much
of laziness as of the time-consuming care which went into his works, and of the high standard
he set himself. He produced all too few paintings—but too many for most of his short life to
have been spent in 'low piss-pot taverns'.

Brouwer was born in Oudenaarde, in Flanders, in 1605 or in January 1606. So much is certain. When his father died he was sixteen years old. He seems already to have left his parents'
house by that time, but we do not know when or why he left, or where he went. His father died
penniless—is that why his son left home? The father was also an artist: he designed patterns
(Schablonen—stencils—according to Bode) for carpet weavers. Had he found an assistant in his
gifted son, who received his first instruction from him? It is more than possible: later accounts
indicate such instruction but are ignorant of the family relationship. Where did the boy go
when he left home? One can only guess. He ended up in Holland, either in Amsterdam or in
Haarlem.

Houbraken's narrative deals at length with the years in Holland, especially with the years
of apprenticeship to Frans Hals. The subject offers him an opportunity to depict, in lively
black and white, an unattractive Hals contrasted to a sympathetically presented, talented
young rowdy. Whether this is unjust to the great Haarlem master apparently does not matter
to the writer. Houbraken's biographical sketch of Hals transforms him into something of a

caricature. The times knew little of nuance in describing people: not individuals, but stereotyped figures were set over against one another. Shakespeare alone, perhaps, had offered real people to his audiences. A drunkard or a miser was simply a drunkard or a miser, characterized by stereotyped attributes. This is all the more perplexing when an impressive body of masterpieces has been left behind, as in the case of Hals or Brouwer.[1] Who can reconcile Hals' Laughing Cavalier in the Wallace Collection with Houbraken's image of Hals? The brilliant waistcoat, painted so surely, clearly, and exactly, with such certainty, such disciplined energy, is this the work of a man who, dead drunk, had to be undressed and put to bed every evening by his pupils?

Martin considers Hals not very productive in these years.[2] He is credited with having produced only two group portraits of the civic guards, and twenty-seven other portraits between the years 1620 and 1630. But what paintings these are! What work must have gone into the costumes of velvet, brocade, satin, and silk. The gold embroidery, jewelry, enormous lace collars and cuffs are all rendered with finesse and precision, yet with such apparent ease. He also painted many small genre scenes in the twenties: not only heads of children (perhaps his own) exquisitely and fluently rendered, but also such an accomplished, entirely original composition as the Merry Company in the Metropolitan Museum in New York. Here rapid, free, broad 38 brushwork combines with clear-cut definition of form, able rendering of materials, and deliberate composition. It is painted with passion—the passion of an artist, not a drunkard—and is governed throughout by a sense of artistic responsibility. Everywhere it is frank and fresh, sparkling and exhilarating, but at the same time surprisingly refined and sensitive in tone. Here we are face to face with the work of the chosen master and precursor of Adriaen Brouwer, who must have joined him shortly after it was painted. Deeply under the influence of Hals' grandiose art and technical proficiency, he was to interpret the example in a fashion entirely his own.

The sea voyage on which Brouwer was captured by pirates and lost all his clothes (unless it is the invention of his biographers) must have preceded this apprenticeship. Perhaps it happened on the journey from Flanders to Holland: he arrives in Amsterdam destitute, and dresses

(¹) In Houbraken's pages there is gross unfairness in the way in which Hals, set off against Brouwer, is severely criticized without any mention of his eminent qualities as a painter. The inaccuracies and inconsistencies are obvious: He was known to his guileless apprentices primarily as a drunk and a stingy cheat; he exploited and starved them, while selling their work for his own gain; and his wife was his evil genius. Altogether he is supposed to have been a nasty, grumbling hypocrite. Now Hals was certainly no saint, but the face he shows in his work is jovial and animated. The genre-like pictures he painted of his many children reveal a tender-hearted man who could appreciate the freshness of childhood. Either Houbraken was misinformed, or else he gave in unscrupulously to the desire to dish up an interesting story. Hals' pupils appear, in the biography devoted to Hals—among other places—full of concern for him, which indicates another sort of relationship! Hals would certainly not have behaved as an exploiting skinflint only toward Brouwer, begrudging him a good suit of clothes (he was responsible for clothing his apprentices). Or was it that Brouwer had no parents to stand up for him?

(²) W. Martin, De Hollandsche Schilderkunst in de Zeventiende Eeuw, Vol. 1 (Amsterdam, n.d.).

11

himself in sackcloth, which he has painted profusely with flowers, and varnished. Thus dressed he goes out, and, in the street his clothes catch the attention and fancy of the ladies. He wanders 'into a comedy playing in the Academy at Amsterdam' (de Bie) where he makes a speech and is generally admired. He then rubs all the paint off with a wet rag, and, in a sort of moral peroration scoffs at those who admired his clothing.

This may have been a traditional tale, but it fits the son of a man who drew designs for carpet weavers—the word 'carpet' (tapijt) bringing to mind here not floor-coverings, but richly worked wall-hangings, and perhaps the gorgeously embroidered clothing such as we come upon in Hals' paintings. Houbraken, who knew nothing of the elder Brouwer's occupation, has another story which attests to Adriaen's familiarity with this kind of work: 'Brouwer, while still young, was kept in by his mother to draw leaf work and birds in ink on linen. She went over these designs with thread, and made them up into bonnets and bodices to sell to farmers' wives.' Frans Hals is said to have passed the house, and thus to have discovered the young artist. Although it is known that Brouwer's mother lived in Oudenaarde, still one can see in this story an echo of the sort of work with which Brouwer's career began. The curious thing is that we find in Brouwer's known works no trace of this facility for painting such motifs.

Adriaen is said to have run away from his master. Whether this really happened, and whether it was because Hals and his wife exploited and starved him, is very doubtful: it fits too neatly into the schematic picture which Houbraken wished to draw of Brouwer as the genius-rake. According to Houbraken's narrative, Brouwer goes to Amsterdam, where he falls in with Barent van Someren, the art-loving inn-keeper, 'in 't Schild van Frankrijk'. Van Someren discovers that Adriaen is the mysterious 'foreign' painter whose work Hals has been selling for his own profit. The image of the young libertine is conjured up, and a traditional story added, to the effect that he took part in the siege of Breda in 1625 on the side of the States of Holland. (A map of the siege was later found among his paltry possessions, probably the famous large print by Jacques Callot.)

Another picturesque episode from Houbraken falls in this period, after Brouwer's departure from Haarlem: word has spread quickly that Brouwer is the young artist whose works Hals has been offering for sale, and that he has established himself in Amsterdam. Collectors now seek after his work. Meanwhile van Someren has urged him to undertake a large canvas in place of many small ones, and so he paints a tavern fight over cards between peasants and soldiers.[1] Among the collectors is du Vermandois, who looks at the big picture and asks its

(1) Hofstede de Groot thought, as he writes in the Introduction to his 'Kritisches Verzeichnis', that he had located this painting among Brouwer's works in the Pinakothek in Munich; but the description does not tally; the Munich painting is certainly from the Antwerp period. It is questionable whether Brouwer, during his Holland period, would have treated a subject so typical of his later work. Would there have been soldiers lounging about taverns in Holland at this time?

price. Brouwer hesitates, but egged on by van Someren, risks asking the unheard-of price of one hundred ducatons. Du Vermandois accepts, and takes Brouwer to his own house to pay him the money. Brouwer returns with his mint of money, throws the silver on his bed, and 'rolls in it'. Then he puts it in his pocket and disappears for nine days. When he comes to the surface, still in good spirits, and is asked where the money is, he replies that 'he has got rid of the ballast'.

Brouwer to a T—at least as he appears in these colourful old stories. It would have been quite a feat to squander one hundred ducatons with the purchasing power of that time, in nine days. He could hardly have done it by himself; although, as will appear later, he was second to none in this respect.

Three facts are known about this period. On July the twenty-third, 1626, the twenty-year old Brouwer declared before a notary that he had seen certain paintings in Amsterdam in March, 1625. His opinion, then, had some official value. We are dealing with a precocious young man! In the same year, 1626, he was a member of the Haarlem 'Rederijkerskamer', 'In Liefde Boven Al'. He occupied himself with verse, as appears from a short poem in praise of a longer one commemorating the Battle of Pavia. The former, written by the poet Pieter Nootmans of Amsterdam was dedicated on March 10th, 1627, to the 'skilful and world-famous young Adriaen Brouwer'. It is no small matter for a twenty-one or twenty-two-year-old man to be publicly praised in such words in a poem. Much can be inferred from these facts, although little about his art: between 1625 and 1626 he moved, or rather returned, from Amsterdam to Haarlem. So he worked there not only as a student. He must have been studying with Hals before his twentieth year; he must have gone to Amsterdam in or about 1625, and subsequently returned to Haarlem, no longer as a student, but as, among other things, a member of the 'Rederijkerskamer'. He apparently enjoyed respect in both cities, not only as a painter, but as a man of letters as well; and it follows that he was not without spiritual culture. One cannot, therefore, identify him with the people he liked to paint, any more than one can infer that Bruegel was a peasant because he painted peasants! He subsequently maintained this level, as appears from The Smokers in New York—he is one of those men who radiate genius, and not only in his own field. From the beginning he exhibits an unexampled insight into his fellow-men, a psychological inquisitiveness and understanding, which reminds one of Shakespeare and Rembrandt. The fact that he was both a painter and a poet is not his only similarity to the versatile Gerbrand Adriaensz. Bredero, who was his elder by twenty years, and who lived only one year longer than Brouwer. But comparing Bredero's poems with Brouwer's scenes, one finds that Brouwer's more heavily laboured work displays, in place of the generalized types of Bredero's light comedy, an empathy and an individualization unusual for the time. Already in the Holland period, individual characterization was replacing the steriotypes which Brouwer, too, had originally painted. Bredero found a like-minded illustrator in Willem

Buytewegh, whose nickname, 'Witty William', suited him so perfectly; Brouwer's paintings, however, cannot be put into words.

From these records it appears that during his years in Holland the young man from Oudenaarde had developed into an independent and acknowledged master. This period closed not later than the end of 1631, when he was twenty-five or twenty-six years old. But this chronology leaves no place for all sorts of second-rate, crude and clumsy work at the beginning of his career: the much sought-after paintings which Hals offered for sale as the work of a foreign master can hardly have been of this sort. Moreover, a development from these stiff and unimaginative products to the refined and delicate art of Brouwer is not psychologically acceptable.

We find him in Antwerp in 1631. What had moved him to go there is not known.[1] In the winter of 1631/32 he is known to have paid the entire subscription fee of a master in the St. Luke's Guild at Antwerp, and in the same guild-year an apprentice, Jean Baptiste d'Andois, had already been articled to him. From this it appears that his status as master was acknowledged. This is also evident from a statement which van den Branden discusses, dated March the fourth, 1632, by 'Signor Adriaen Brouwer, painter residing within this city of Antwerp', drawn up for the benefit of the seller of the painting Peasants Dancing; Brouwer said here that he had painted this picture, acquired by Rubens the year before, only once; from which we may conclude that Brouwer probably painted it before arriving in Antwerp, where his fame had preceded him. Rubens would then have bought it early in 1631—not from Brouwer personally. Ultimately Rubens acquired seventeen paintings by Brouwer.[2] He must have set more than a little value on an original and unique Brouwer, and felt obliged to protect himself from repetitions or copies.

Brouwer even drew a composition sketch of the painting on the reverse side of this instrument, which is so remarkable in many respects. The statement was given before the notary Pieter de Breuseghem at the request of the art dealer Captain Daniel Deegbroot. On the same occasion he swore to the authenticity of another of his works on behalf of the Antwerp dealer Jacomo de Cachiopin. These dealers appear to have availed themselves of Brouwer's presence in their city to obtain declarations from him. This suggests that he had settled there only a short time before, that—and this is noteworthy—one had to have protection against copies of his works, and that (writes van den Branden) 'even then hucksters tried to smuggle fakes into the art world'.

The expression 'Signor Adriaen Brouwer' suggests an esteem which is difficult to reconcile with the image of a seedy vagabond, finding refuge in low taverns. But he was certainly no comfortable, substantial burgher. In the summer of 1632 a creditor had an inventory of his

[1] On p. 15 Bode says that between 1628 and 1631 nothing is known of the artist; but he does not state what is known of the year 1628. [2] See Appendix B.

14

possessions drawn up, and a poor showing it was[1]: in the way of furniture, a small mirror only; a pair of breeches, two coats, one of which was trimmed with silver, a cloak of broadcloth, three black caps, two hats, two sets of sleeves and a simple assortment of linen: five cuffs, a collar and a shirt. This presumably does not include what he was wearing at the time, since shoes are not mentioned. The appearance of a 'signor' could apparently be maintained with this outfit—and he could make sure in his mirror. There was also a modest collection of painter's gear (but no fewer than fifty-four brushes and a lay figure), a few paintings—including two by the sixteenth-century master Cornelis van Cleve—prints, the above-mentioned map of the siege of Breda, and eight books—a quite creditable number for the time.

Why then those debts, when he had no trouble selling his works and could command good prices? Again, there is an attractive story: if Brouwer could not pay the bill in an inn, he would make sketches and offer them to the innkeeper as payment, or send him off to the collectors with them. If the latter would not pay his prices, Brouwer would put the sketches in the fire. The destitute 'signor' still had his pride. His attitude even reminds us of such a type as Bredero's 'Spaanse Brabander', except that we must see Brouwer as an exceptionally talented, hard-working and serious artist, against the solid background of a workshop. It does not seem likely that Brouwer's finely finished paintings were produced in inns—nor in the 'piss-pot taverns' of which the epitaph speaks: there he would not have run up so large a bill. But he would undoubtedly have visited disreputable places hunting for his types and motifs. According to van den Branden, Brouwer 'became one of the pillars' of 'de Robijn' (the tavern the Ruby) in the Wiegstraat.

The tavern keeper, Gijsbrecht van den Cruijse, was a first-rate artist-tempter. He must have been a good talker, since he was a 'rederijker', and was even chosen Deacon of the 'Kamer de Goudsbloem'. By means of this title he lured members of the chamber into his tavern. But more ensnaring than his talk were the drinks which he poured out for the artists, sometimes without requiring hard cash in payment. Instead, this unprincipled Maecenas would accept paintings, and he came to have quite a collection: one could always come and admire them, displayed in one of his rooms, the walls of which were covered with leather stamped in gold and green. No fewer than twenty-three landscapes by Joos de Momper were there, and after his death this famous artist still owed van den Cruijse four hundred and eighty-three guilders and six stivers. Also to be seen there was 'a small picture by the painter Brouwer, of Tobacco Drinkers, in an oval ebony frame'; and on page ninety-nine of the debt book, 'Signor Brouwer the painter' was down for thirty-two guilders and thirteen stivers, 'which he never settled'.

Apparently he could spend lavishly and pay with his paintings—but this conscientious, delicate and slow painter was not able to finish paintings fast enough.

[1] See Appendix C.

15

On February the twenty-third, 1633 Brouwer was a prisoner of the State in the Citadel of Antwerp, where the Spanish garrison was housed. This is a considerable time after his arrival in the city, where he was already a well-known figure, at least in artistic circles. On the twenty-third of September he was still in prison. We do not know why. For debts? Was the Citadel used for debtors? Or was this 'foreigner' from Holland for one reason or another politically suspect? In any case, this is a fine contribution to the picturesque novel of Adriaen Brouwer's life. He was not badly treated. It was possible to mix freely with the people living in the Citadel or having business there—so freely that the prisoner managed to run up a debt of no less than five hundred guilders in those seven months. His creditor, van den Bosch, whom he already owed sixteen hundred guilders, to be paid off in monthly instalments, could not have received any money back while Brouwer was in prison; none the less he gave him five hundred guilders' further credit to meet new debts. Jan van den Bosch, a silk merchant, was, in fact, more a Maecenas than a usurer. He protected Brouwer against his other creditors but, as a good merchant, was careful to put his financial arrangements with the artist in writing before a notary. A large sum of money was involved: at the same time Brouwer had to sign another note for fifteen hundred and sixty guilders borrowed, 'to be paid back in instalments on certain dates, in money or in paintings; with the understanding that, if he does not meet his obligations this time, he will be sued and sentenced mercilessly'.

Accordingly Jan van den Bosch considered the painter worthy of credit although a prisoner. This indicates how highly his paintings were valued, not only for their own sake but as investments as well. (In Rembrandt's difficult years, after his bankruptcy, we encounter the same thing.)

Not only the Spanish soldiers and the inhabitants of the Citadel frequented the tavern. The best Spanish wines were to be had there free of tax, as well as other good things from distant lands. For all that the City Council might prohibit visits, people came and went ... and the prisoner Adriaen Brouwer went deeper into debt.

It was a curious coincidence that both the tavern and the bakery were managed by families which played a role in the artistic life of Antwerp, the Grisons and the Tielens. Baker Tielens married the daughter of the innkeeper Grison, and the Grisons were well-known wood-carvers, later noted for heavily gilded, richly ornamented picture frames popular in England. Hans Tielens, the baker's brother, became a good landscape painter. Baker Tielens was murdered by a colleague from Mechelen, and his daughter, whose mother had died some time before, was seduced by his successor, Joos van Craesbeeck. The girl's grandmother and aunt urged the young baker to marry his victim. He had little inclination to, because of the marriage conditions which these women wished to impose. They were concerned that Joos should profit as little as possible from the blood money, which the murderer paid with great ceremony to the murdered man's mother. The wedding, arrived at in this hardly idyllic way, took place on January the twenty-second, 1631; on February the ninth their son was baptized.

Such was the milieu in which Brouwer, as a prisoner, found himself; he would not have been too disconsolate in it. Here a taste for art coincided with a loose style of living and first-rate liquor. The young baker Joos van Craesbeeck became Brouwer's pupil, without giving up his work as a baker. His wife, according to popular report, granted her favours to Adriaen—not improbable in the light of her background. Nor did it hinder the friendship between the master and this pupil of his own age. At any rate, after his imprisonment Brouwer appears to have made his home with the couple for a short time, when Craesbeeck had established himself as a baker in the city.

And then there is the story of his release from prison—too good to be true, but in keeping with his reputation. No less a person than the Duke of Arenberg was also a prisoner in the Citadel. He was allowed to walk about 'freely'—between two soldiers—and happened to go by Brouwer's cell. Brouwer took him for the governor and begged to be released, pleading innocence. Arenberg inquired who he was; when Brouwer said he was a painter, Arenberg asked for proof. Later the same afternoon when the great Rubens came to visit Arenberg, the latter asked him to provide painting equipment, so as to put Brouwer to the test. It came the following evening, and Brouwer set to work and painted a small canvas which is described in some detail by Houbraken. (Traditionally this has been wrongly identified with the fine painting in the Museum in Brussels of a group of men sitting round a table outside an inn.) Arenberg 'was greatly pleased by it'. A few days later Rubens asked about the painter. When he saw the painting, he exclaimed, 'Upon my soul, it is Brouwer's', and offered six hundred guilders for it, but Arenberg would not part with it. Brouwer 'had been arrested by the soldiers and taken to prison merely on the suspicion that he was a spy.' Rubens went to the governor and gave his word that Brouwer was not a spy but an able painter; the governor acceded to Rubens' request. The story, however, is contradictory to all that is known of conditions in the Citadel; and Arenberg was a prisoner there at a later date.

Houbraken's narrative continues:

'Rubens took him home, had a suit of clothes made for him, put him next to him at his table, and took him to call on good people living orderly lives, showing in this way that he held him in high esteem. But the young rapscallion found this style of life a burden, a closer confinement than the prison he had just escaped from. He took to avoiding Rubens, and returned to his former loose living.'

We may conjecture that the great Antwerp master would have liked to have Brouwer associated with his 'house' both from admiration for him and from a desire to play the role of patron to the gifted but rakish twenty-six-year-old artist. It is difficult to imagine the grandeur and the courtly style in which 'the painter of princes and the prince of painters' lived, surrounded by co-workers—themselves reputable artists—, journeymen and apprentices. He had amassed a considerable fortune: the imposing Rubens House in Antwerp is evidence of that. And we know that when his name was submitted to Philip IV for elevation to the hereditary nobility, it was stated that he had sufficient means to lead a life befitting the rank. He received his patent of nobility in 1625, and in 1629 was appointed secretary to the king's 'conseil privé', a well-paid office.

After 1624 he was engaged in State affairs and was sent on a number of diplomatic missions—to the courts of Spain, England and France, among others. Sometimes as an avowed, more often as an unacknowledged agent, using a painting commission to conceal his diplomacy, he negotiated for a truce between the Republic and the Spanish Governors in the South, serving on special missions to Princes Maurice and Frederic Henry. In 1630 he was knighted in Whitehall by Charles I and was presented with costly gifts, a sword, a ring and a chain. At fifty-three he married the sixteen-year-old Hélène Fourment: when he had been advised to choose a lady from courtly circles, his reply was that he preferred to have a wife who would not blush when he took up his palette. (This was not the only reason why he chose young Hélène: she was considered [by circles both inside and outside the court] the most beautiful of women, and was a kind of show-piece for her husband.) And thus Rubens, living between two worlds, ought certainly to be included in the courtly sphere. He must have been particularly offended by a letter of 1633 from the Duke of Arenberg, in which he was flatly told that he was not the latter's 'kind'. After this his glory as a diplomat seems to have waned somewhat, and in the same year these activities came to an end. In the first years of Brouwer's stay in Antwerp, however, his income and his reputation still appear to have been intact.

We can assume that Adriaen Brouwer, independent and proud, would have had little desire to be patronized by this exalted colleague thirty years his senior; Rubens, because of this difference in age, would have been likely to adopt a protective manner toward him. Brouwer's refusal did not stop Rubens, as we have said, from adding seventeen of his works to his very carefully selected collection (which contained ten paintings by Bruegel the Elder); (Appendix B). Houbraken, indeed, observes that the restraints of Rubens' social surroundings would have cramped his style of living. But Rubens' artistic environment may have been an even greater restraint: Brouwer, perhaps deliberately, always kept at a proper distance from it. He found his subjects in an entirely different world. (Rubens' admiration for his work is all the more telling because of this.) Brouwer's method, too, was contrary to Rubens'. One can hardly imagine Adriaen having his compositions executed by journeymen: the essential elements would have suffered, certainly in his own eyes. Rubens could, without damage, leave much to others; time and again he had to promise, in contracts with those who commissioned his paintings, to do the entire work himself. His style was based on grandeur, breadth and vigour; the technique required a great deal of experience but, being based on a system, could be learned by a good craftsman. The opposite is the case with the younger artist. A style so thoroughly personal, with its precision, colour, treatment of light and tonality, a style continuously changing in response to circumstance—such a style would not brook the collaboration of others.

Too close a bond with this 'master' would not do, for it would entail some measure of subjection. Brouwer preferred a complete freedom, which would not rule out a friendly relationship or at least some contact. In one field, landscape painting, there is certainly some connection between their styles. In his later years, after the acquisition, in 1635, of his large estate and castle, 'Het Steen', near Mechelen, Rubens painted more and more landscapes. These were direct representations of observed reality, unlike the immense, imaginative conceptions of the cosmos which he had painted earlier. At the same time that Rubens began to paint these small, simple canvases, which hitherto had seemed to lie outside his province, Brouwer was also painting his small landscapes, so wonderfully sensitive and intimate. Did Brouwer influence Rubens?[1] There are remarkable points of agreement, but the change to more modest, intimate work can also be related to the fact that Rubens in later life suffered from gout in his hands. Rubens found his subjects in his beautiful estate in the neighbourhood of Mechelen, with its broad fields and woodland stretching into the distance, and its small castle accurately portrayed again and again. Brouwer, on the other hand, turned to the bleak dunes of the Kempen, with their scraggy trees; they were to be found to the immediate north of Antwerp, in Cappellen, Heyde and Kalmpthout.[2]

If not with Rubens, did Brouwer after his release from prison go to live with van Craesbeeck and his seductive young wife? Possibly; but not for long, for in April 1634 he made his home with the well-known engraver Paul du Pont (Paulus Pontius). The latter reproduced Rubens' compositions in peerless prints, and is accordingly to be reckoned within Rubens' sphere. The house is situated in Everdijstraat. The neighbourhood is quiet and rather dignified, in the centre of the city and only a five-minute walk from the imposing Rubens House.

Here were surroundings to Brouwer's liking. On the spot, (in the taverns, that is, which he

[1] The question of the influence of the younger artist on the elder has already been raised by Max Rooses ('Rubens', p. 616) and answered in this way: 'Nous croyons que Rubens était accessible à toutes les influences et à tous les enseignements, et qu'il peut avoir appris à l'école de Brouwer comme à celle du Titien.'

[2] Dr. M. E. Tralbout has pointed out to me that the landscapes Brouwer painted are to be found in these regions; and that the farm house with the thatched roof in the painting in Berlin has striking similarities to the houses in three paintings from St. Rémy by Vincent van Gogh (B.d.l.F. 691, 692, 693). Van Gogh writes of these paintings in his letters. They are, he says, recollections of the North, and he particularly mentions Kalmpthout, a place 'where I should have liked to work for a while.'

painted,) he made only sketches; in his studio he composed the final work, where he was free to arrange the scene as he thought best. There are few paintings among his known works, even among the smallest and simplest, which are not finished with the greatest care. The sketches may have been finished in the studio; the more complicated paintings certainly were. The more mature, perfect, richly peopled canvases required his full concentration and the quiet of a studio; just as the master engraver du Pont would have produced his work in peaceful surroundings, conducive to the perfection and fineness required by the technique. Continuous variation in the method of execution is a hallmark of Brouwer's paintings. The actual painting process, the purely technical operation, was for him the most fascinating side of his craft and aroused his artistic passion. In this respect he can be compared with Rembrandt: each work is a new task, a new problem to be tackled with renewed attention, love and dedication, and to be finished to the smallest details. This requires the quiet of a studio, and slow painting. No one could paint like this in a pot-house where a pair of furious card players are murderously attacking each other, a soldier draws his rapier, a drunkard lies vomiting on the floor; nor can one imagine these people posing in these positions for Brouwer! He had a lay figure for reconstructing one or another position. It is even less likely that those surgeons and their ministering wives, who are dressing a head-, shoulder- or foot-wound with intense concentration, posed for Brouwer with their writhing patients. And yet how sharply every role, every exact mental attitude is portrayed in these compositions. The evidence obliges us to represent the master, not yet thirty years old, absorbed in a labour which required quiet and concentrated attention.

Our high-spirited, raffish young 'prankster' ('potsig' is the term used continuously by Houbraken) felt the need for relaxation, the more, perhaps, as his work required intense concentration. This sort of solace cost more than his slow, difficult work paid: he always took his pleasures in a far different kind of tavern and environment than those he painted. With his friends he went to the better—and more expensive—places, such as Gijsbrecht van den Cruijse's 'de Robijn' in the Wiegstraat. Van Dyck's portrait of Brouwer shows a swank young man with festive moustachios and an unkempt head of hair. (The original [?] water colour from which Schelte à Bolswert made his etching, is in the collection of the Duke of Buccleugh.) According to van Dyck's custom, it is somewhat idealized; but not so as to present a misleading image of the subject. In such wise can we imagine the threadbare gentleman . . . who had, among his scant possessions, a mirror in which to cultivate his appearance . . . just like the 'Spaanse Brabander'. He looks old for his years—no wonder! He appears haughty; and the reports of his pranks indicate an arrogant and scornful young man, untroubled by self-doubts. And it is van Dyck who depicts him so—van Dyck, above all the portraitist of the eminent and courtly of his time. His haughtiness seems to hide an almost despondent nature.

20

This does not come altogether as a surprise, in that his pictures, with all their objectivity and rawness, are not basically funny. No moralist, he only recorded facts; but consider the facts he chose and the way he stated them. Bullart tells a characteristic story which illustrates his sardonic turn of mind, his bold arrogance and his rashness and wastefulness as well. The story is in some ways analogous to the one told above of how he appeared at the Academy at Amsterdam. As the same story appears in van den Branden:

'[Brouwer noticed] that his relatives (then he did have relatives in Antwerp?) despised him because he dressed with little taste and was sometimes even slovenly. So he had a velvet suit made, of the latest style worn by the great Antwerp merchants. One of his cousins, who was going to be married shortly, hurried to invite him to the wedding, for such a well-dressed gentleman would honour the company. But when the whole party praised him at table for the magnificence and cleanliness of his clothes, he suddenly took two dishes of meat with greasy gravy which he smeared over his costly garment, declaring that his clothes should enjoy the meal, since they, not he, had been invited. Having in this way shown the astonished onlookers that he despised them all because they set more value on the outer than the inner man, he threw his soiled clothes into the fire and returned to the inn to find more honest friends along with the tobacco, wine and gambling to which he was already addicted.'

It is because of his debts that he comes up time and again in the Antwerp archives. He appeared before a notary with his friend and landlord Paul du Pont, whom he owed the sizeable sum of two hundred and ninety-seven guilders, for nine months' board and moneys borrowed (so it seems that he boarded with du Pont). Out of his scanty collection of paintings he had to surrender to du Pont a small painting by 'de Sotte Cleve', a panel by van Dyck and moreover one of his own works, a brothel scene, on which he was still at work. The engraver Peter de Jode was a witness on this occasion; his name appears repeatedly with du Pont's and Brouwer's, suggesting a more or less close relationship among the three artists.

There were also relations with the courtly and elegant van Dyck. The latter thought him worth including in his great iconography of 'princes, scholars, painters, sculptors and connoisseurs of the art of painting', whom he portrayed generally in water colour grisaille. The portrait of Brouwer bears, at least in the fifth state, the inscription 'Adrianus Brauwer, Gryllorum pictor Antverpiae.' (In the second state he is called 'Abraham' by mistake, and in the sixth 'Brauwer' is substituted by 'Brouwer'.) The series did not appear in print until 1646, several years after the death of both Brouwer and van Dyck, which explains the original errors and perhaps as well the banal title 'Gryllorum pictor', painter of caprices;[1] in which case it would not be an appreciation by van Dyck himself.

(1) 'Grylli' was with the Romans a name for comic genre pieces. (cf. Wilh. Schmidt, Das Leben des Malers Adrian Brouwer, Leipzig 1873, p. 7, note).

Thus the circle of those in the midst of whom we see Brouwer widens. In 1635 Jan Lievens came to Antwerp from London, where he had gone from Leiden in 1632. Brouwer established close relations with him, as well as with another Dutch painter, Jan Davidz. de Heem. On the first of March, 1636, Brouwer and de Heem appeared as witnesses to a deed in which Lievens took on a fifteen-year-old apprentice, and made a contract with his mother. (The contract was for six years: everything that the apprentice was to paint in that time would belong to Lievens; in return Lievens was to provide tuition, bed and board, and linen and clothing as well during the last three years. His mother was to look after his laundry and, for two guilders a month, after Lievens' also!)

Lievens came from a background similar to Brouwer's. The son of a Ghent embroiderer, he was one or two years younger. For a few years before 1632 he worked with Rembrandt and, as a consequence came under the strong and spirited influence of that great master. There are remains of this in his art, and in his conceptions as well: did he perhaps own some of Rembrandt's works? Rembrandt, we know, greatly admired the slightly older Brouwer; would Brouwer have been altogether unaware of Rembrandt?[1] Brouwer's work does show a definite relationship to the latter's. The refined art of painting, with its delicate gradations of light and dark, with its fine nuances of colour and preference for pale grey, lilac and violet, with its stippled flecks of glancing light—this art was practiced nowhere as in Rembrandt's studio in Leiden. These qualities come to the fore in Brouwer's painting first in his Antwerp period. Was Lievens perhaps the intermediary? He had left Rembrandt at the moment when this style was reaching its apex in such a painting as the Rape of Proserpine (in Berlin). Surely Lievens was acquainted with this work. Lievens was somewhat younger than Brouwer; it is not very likely that he had much influence on the older painter. He had shown himself in Leiden to be, on the contrary, so susceptible to the influence of his master that some of his works have been ascribed to Rembrandt (and surely not the other way around). But perhaps Brouwer was indirectly influenced by Rembrandt, the creative genius whose artistry was

[1] A personal encounter between the two masters, such as takes place in Felix Timmermans' novel about Brouwer, must be regarded as out of the question. Brouwer had already gone to Antwerp when Rembrandt went, at first only temporarily, from Leiden to Amsterdam, to paint the Anatomy Lesson of Dr. Tulp. He would not have received the Amsterdam commission, unless he already had a good name there; but Brouwer, working in Haarlem, need not have known of him. This visit paid by Brouwer to Rembrandt is one of many fictions in the novel by Timmermans (1946). For all that the author has not pretended to give an historically accountable picture, such a method is questionable when applied to the historical figure of Brouwer. There is something suggestive in the images and atmosphere created by Timmermans, and the reader finds it difficult to free himself from this representation, all the more because it is sometimes based on historical facts; for the novel is an elaboration of Houbraken's narrative. Timmermans shies away from taking over the disreputable character of Hals, whom he thinks better of as an artist than did Houbraken—but he is correspondingly more severe in his judgment of Hals' wife. The character of Craesbeeck is crabbedly overdrawn; nor does Jordaens come off very happily. This misrepresentation of historical figures leads to the formation of legends.

always to be perceived, however faint, under the surface of Lievens' painting. The difference in ages between Rembrandt and Brouwer was at the most a year and a half.[1] The Dutchman became a great admirer of the Fleming: he appears according to his inventory in 1656 to have owned eight of his paintings and an album of his drawings (portefeuille).

Lievens drew a beautiful sketch of Brouwer (now in the collection of Frits Lugt[2]). There is 35 further evidence that the two painters from Holland saw something of each other. In his early years at Leiden in the sphere of Rembrandt, Lievens had failed to fulfil Huygens' great expectations of him. After that van Dyck's elegant example was harmful. Now he was painting landscapes, a few of which, indeed, were once ascribed to Brouwer. A relationship similar to the one with Rembrandt had developed.

The Metropolitan Museum 'Smokers' (formerly in the Steengracht Collection in The Hague) V appears to be identical with a painting of men smoking and drinking described by Campo Weyerman in his 'Levensbeschrijvinge', Vol. I, p. 69 (1729 edition).[3] In this case the painters Jan Davidsz. de Heem, Jan Koessiers and Brouwer himself are represented. The three cavaliers shown might perfectly well be painters, and the figure on the right is surely a portrait. Carousing in a drab inn of a sort frequented by drunks and tobacco smokers, they have been joined by a type who is more at home in such places. The latter appears to be drawing attention from a companion with a roguish expression, in the left of the scene. This fellow is sitting on his haunches, making a gesture which both suggests a practical joke and exhorts the onlookers not to give him away. The large smoker in the foreground would be Brouwer, agreeing in type with the portrait by van Dyck. The man on the right bears a resemblance to the portrait that Lievens drew of J. D. de Heem. This identification is consistent with Weyerman's[4].

This work, then, is an important document about Brouwer. As one would expect, his bearing and expression here distinguish him from the usual customers of such places, although he is more relaxed and seems to be enjoying his surroundings more than his comrade de Heem in his correct black outfit with white collar and cuffs. But then the latter had only been in Antwerp since 1635 or 1636.

The inference would be that Brouwer did not visit these questionable places only to make sketches. We discover him in this picture indulging his weakness for the pipe and the bottle. True, it is not the shabbiest of the places that the painter introduces us to. Moreover, must this

[1] If Brouwer was thirty-two years old at the time of his death in January, 1638, he must have been born between January, 1605 and January, 1606; Rembrandt was born on July fifteenth, 1606.
[2] Mentioned by H. Schneider in 'Festschrift Friedländer', 1927.
[3] Schneider, 'Festschrift', p. 272.
[4] The untenable identification of the figures as Frans Hals (right), Adriaen van Ostade (behind the cloud of smoke) and Brouwer himself is considered in the discussion of the painting in Part II.

scene, obviously composed and painted in the studio, be a portrayal of an actual event? Brouwer was surely capable of freely altering the facts in order to bring out the different types and characters yet more clearly.

The inn in the picture is outside the city: the view through the top half of the door is of a country road by a farm, a bit of nature that could be a fragment of a Brouwer landscape. The work might well have been a merry souvenir of an excursion made by the three comrades to the district where Brouwer found so many of his motifs. The view of the country road tells us a little more about Brouwer's way of life. His inns are often village ones: the city dweller turned to the country, finding his inspiration there—and a place to rest, eat and drink as well. For in all likelihood these were not one-day trips. There were dunes not far outside Antwerp, but it would have been a walk of several hours to reach them in the neighbourhood of Kalmpthout—to the north, accordingly—where Brouwer worked out the ideas that took his fancy; and there was work to be done before returning to town. The particularly small format of Brouwer's landscapes suggests that they may have been painted on the spot, contrary to the customary method at the time, and this would account for their singular atmospheric freshness. He would, then, have frequented the village taverns, where he fell in with vagrant country people and disreputable characters from the nearby port. There he saw scenes which he would sketch on the spot and later, at home in his studio, work into completed, vivid pictures with a fascinating story. Sometimes his friends came along, and the day would turn into a festival—and Brouwer would take ironic pleasure in making de Heem feel somewhat less at home than Brouwer himself did. Lievens, who was painting similar landscapes in the same small size, occasionally would have accompanied him, and so would the slightly younger Teniers.

Bullart writes:

'Comme il avoit l'esprit facétieux et porté à la débauche il en fit paroistre les traits dans ses mœurs aussi bien que dans ses ouvrages. Brouwer estoit extrèmement addonné au tabac et à l'Eau de vie. Comme il n'aimait que le libertinage et la boisson, il se négligeait jusqu'au point que d'estre le plus souvent couvert d'un méchant habit, qui le rendoit méprisable à ceux qui ne savaient pas combien il excelloit en l'Art, et qui ne pénétroient pas plus avant que l'extérieur. Il travaillait rarement ailleurs que dans le Cabaret.'

This account, in the 'Académie des Sciences et des Arts', was published in 1682, but had been written much earlier. Would Brouwer have so gone down in his last years? The paintings already mentioned belie such a picture, as does the fact that he joined the 'rederijkerskamer' 'de Violieren' of St. Luke's Guild with his friends du Pont and de Jode for the guild year 1634/35. On September the eighteenth, 1637, four months before his death, he paid his fee of ten guilders. Moreover he kept his friends to the end of his life. The picture of himself in the above-mentioned canvas in New York, which cannot have been painted before 1635, since de Heem figures in it, points to a social position a few years before his death in January, 1638, far more favourable than Bullart describes.

The story of Brouwer at his cousin's wedding feast does not tally with this passage from Bullart and does not suggest any such dissolution. Where did Bullart get his facts? He lived in Brussels, where Craesbeeck also lived in his later years. These old historians did not hesitate to repeat gossip. He may have consulted Craesbeeck. Perhaps the latter furnished a picture of his former friend and master—and his wife's lover—which was somewhat more picturesque and melodramatic than the reality warranted. Bullart for his part may have amplified the fascinating facts about the talented artist who died young after a life of dissipation and of wasted genius. Such a biographer would not have been too much constrained by the obligations of historical responsibility. There may have been some foundation in fact underlying these tales; but it is also clear that Brouwer maintained to the end of his life both the standards of his art and his friendships in artistic circles. He was overburdened with debts; but his company as an artist was valued, apart from conversation and revelry. He appears to have been living in du Pont's house when he died, and the fact that he was in debt does not seem to have carried much weight with the engraver. Immediately after his death there was a lawsuit over a 'false' Brouwer (March the twenty-fourth, 1638); and five creditors turned up, claiming a share in his effects. The latter probably consisted of the paintings which he had left behind, with a real value. Among the creditors were his earlier pupil Jan Dandoy (who had become a master in 1637) and also Jan de Heem.

Bullart's narrative becomes still sadder:

'Il mourut à Anvers âgé de trente-deux ans seulement, consommé de débauches, et si pauvre qu'il fallut mandier l'assistance des personnes charitables pour fournir aux frais de son enterrement. Il fût inhumé dans l'ambulance des P. P. Carmes d'Anvers; d'où il a esté depuis transporté dans leur Eglise; non pour ses vertus, mais à cause de la grande réputation qu'il a remportée par son pinceau.'

He died at the end of January, 1638, and was buried in the church of the Carmelite monastery on the first of February. Apparently his body was first put in a common grave outside the church, because no one knew who he was. When his identity became known, he was given a simple burial for eighteen stivers.

All sorts of tales collected around his death; one was that he had fled to Paris on account of his debts—or, it is sometimes suggested, for other reasons; he returned, exhausted by his debauchery, to die only two days later; but this is no more than vague rumour. Also it is said that he died of the plague: this supposition should not be entirely dismissed, and would shed light on the manner of his first burial.

He was thirty-two: a young and intense life was cut off; of its intensity there is no doubt. It is apparent in the exquisite, brilliantly effective drawings (all too rare), which are a surprising contrast to the painstaking delicacy of most of the paintings. But the perfect finish of the paintings is also a product of Brouwer's tense absorption in his work. So too the deeply felt pity in the penetrating characterization of his subjects, who are made to reveal their natures in their momentary actions.

A life of ever-renewed vigour: the prerequisite of his work. Without it, how could he have achieved such perfection of technical control, representation of milieu and aesthetic scrupulousness in so little time? Already in his Dutch period he appeared as an accomplished master of his craft. This, however, leaves no time for continuous unbridled dissipation with not only jug and glass, but also with the pipe, the stupifying effect of which he so often depicted.

The tobacco then smoked was by no means harmless, and had results far more serious than today's. With an altogether different end in view, it was 'sucked' from little earthenware pipes. There are many paintings in which men are shown sitting, as in an opium den, with pipes in their hands, staring dully at the ceiling as if in trance.[1] This effect explains the opposition of the magistrates and the church to its use. Only if he had observed them, could Brouwer have painted these baneful effects so convincingly; he may even have tried the drug himself.[2]

The painting of The Smokers in New York, with Brouwer as the principal figure, can hardly provide an exact account of his way of life. It would not have embarrassed him to paint himself in a role more active, more depraved than was the actual case. The full emphasis of the painting falls on the different conditions of the three artists: De Heem is a bit doped, but has control of himself: he sits quietly, decorously filling his pipe. Koessiers is already in a trance, as Brouwer painted so many smokers. He himself is in worse shape still, looking downwards with curiously wide-open eyes. He gives himself a more active—and not very attractive—part.

He could portray himself in any way he wished, but did not have the same license concerning the others. How much of this was braggadocio? One must beware of jumping to conclusions. The fourth rascal is a splendid type, used to heavy drinking. Although he is not sober, his role calls for presence of mind, since he has to engage the attention of the others while number five brings off his practical joke. How perfectly each fulfils his role in this little comedy; and for just that reason one cannot infer too much about the daily lives of these artists.

These exciting tales about such a rough, gay life with its debts, prison and an early wretched death in extreme poverty are difficult to check; so that Felix Timmermans could sketch a mot-

---

(1) Probably hemp was added to plain tobacco to induce narcosis and ecstasy. (The eastern narcotic 'hashish' is extracted from hemp.) Hemp was commonly grown in Flanders. Felix Timmermans describes its use; he calls the mixture 'belladonna': desired by addicts and forbidden under severe penalties, it was smoked in secret taverns.

(2) This is not to say, however, that anyone who was painted in the seventeenth century with a pipe in his mouth was a drug addict. The narcotic affect depended on the addition of hemp. The smokers painted by Jan Steen and Ostade, for example, show no sign of this.

ley picture with little regard for historical fact. He proposes, in fact, contrasting periods of, on the one hand, concentrated work which left no time for anything else, and, on the other, the wildest orgies, days and nights of gambling, brawling, drinking and erotic pleasures.[1] Surely, this dynamism would not have characterized one side of his being more than the other. His œuvre shows that his intensity drove him to delights of the most noble and delicate flavour and to an ever more profound inner vision. His art was not a trade followed to pay for his revelries. It was his highest passion, to which he dedicated his entire being.

[1] According to Timmermans, Brouwer was as fond of women as of wine. This fits the type that the old stories conjure up; and yet these old stories tell of no love affairs except the one with Craesbeeck's wife, which is supported only by vague rumour. Is this accidental? Love-making is hardly an outstanding feature of Brouwer's works; prostitutes seldom appear, although 'brothel scenes' are continually mentioned in documents, even in the deeds with du Pont which he himself signed; and the women who appear in his paintings are unattractive. In this period the 'brothel scene' was a favourite genre. (One thinks of the paintings by Honthorst and his fellow-Caravaggists of rollicking soldiers and prostitutes, paintings which seem to have been popular in Holland in the twenties.) Such paintings are not to be found in Brouwer's work. He does occasionally show a fellow putting his hand under a woman's skirts; but the women do not look like prostitutes. Neither do they show great appreciation of the act. The painter's psychological insight into these women is superficial compared with his insight into men and into the older women whom he shows helping surgeons or trying to come between men fighting.

THE DEMARCATION OF BROUWER'S AUTHENTIC WORK

In undertaking a study of Brouwer's life work, we are obliged to sift carefully the list of works ascribed to him. Only a few paintings can be attributed to him on other than stylistic grounds, and not a single drawing. It was exceptional for him to put a monogram on his works—an 'A' and a 'B' joined—and this may equally well have been someone else's doing. There are, to be sure, seventeenth-century prints after his paintings; but few publishers concerned themselves over the authenticity of Brouwer's authorship. The 'Brouwer-look' was enough to justify putting his name on a print, the criterion being type rather than quality. A painting which is similar to a print is not necessarily the model for the print; the painting may itself be a copy of the original—or the print may be after a copy. The object of these prints was their anecdotal content, so that the artistic quality of the original was of no concern.

Brouwer never dated his work; consequently we lack such a starting point for a chronological arrangement. The paintings in the Munich Pinakothek—of an exceptional number—seem to be reliable in quality. But this is not the entire original collection, for a few of the poorer works (now in Aschaffenburg and Regensburg) have been weeded out—and one of the remaining sixteen might well have been given the same treatment (about which more below). The balance does not give a complete picture of Brouwer's art: there are no landscapes, and all the pictures belong to the Antwerp period, owing to the fact that they come from a few collections in the South Netherlands (one of which may have been Rubens'). But the most beautiful landscapes are from this period, as are those pictures, also unrepresented in Munich, with relatively larger figures, such as the surgeon scenes in Frankfort. There is still another group of paintings that must have originated in the Dutch period; they are closely related to each other, but of an intrinsically different character. One can characterize his work in terms of these different types, but this provides no way of distinguishing the work of followers, and copies, from the originals. Quality provides the only possible standard for such discrimination: one must assume that this great artist could not, because of his exceptional devotion to his art and his extreme aesthetic sensibility, fall below a certain level in his work.

There are clearly two major categories to be distinguished in his work, the Dutch period and the Flemish period, scarcely less distinct than van Gogh's Dutch and French periods. The example of van Gogh serves to show how great a distance there can be, even in a short creative period, between early and late works. Both artists exhibit a characteristic spiritual

2. 'PAINTER OF THE LARGE JARS'
PEASANTS CAROUSING
City of York Art Gallery

3. 'PAINTER OF THE LARGE JARS'
THREE MUSICIANS
Rijksmuseum, Amsterdam

4. 'PAINTER OF THE LARGE JARS', SMOKER
Present whereabouts not known

29

growth in an accelerating tempo. The depiction of character in an early Brouwer, as that in the Ruzicka Collection, approaches caricature, as do van Gogh's Potato Eaters. Both artists *then* valued this sort of expression above solely aesthetic considerations, the deliberate and masterful execution of both notwithstanding. For each, concern for purely aesthetic values becomes more operative in the later work, where each seeks a balance between expressionistic meaning and technical artistic achievement. The essential problem for either remains that of expressing the essence of the things portrayed; but at the same time the fact that they are artists and their steadily maturing craftsmanship make ever-increasing demands on the execution.

Although this division is based in Brouwer's case solely on considerations of stylistic criticism, it appears to me to be so convincing, and in view of the circumstances of Brouwer's life, so obvious, that it can be accepted as certain. The work in either group, however, is encumbered with much that does not belong there; and the nature of this ballast is different in either period.

The story of how Hals successfully sold the young Brouwer's work serves to indicate an early appreciation of the artist at the beginning of his Dutch period. Whether it is literally true or not, it must have had some foundation in fact. Since Brouwer had earned himself a name by the time he was twenty, these incidents would have had to take place before 1626. He must already have achieved considerable professional skill, which is not unlikely if we assume that he had been trained in his father's workshop from early childhood on. His departure from home for reasons unknown, in or before his sixteenth year, also argues for an early maturity and confidence in his own artistic ability. His earliest work, consequently, must have evidenced the marks of precocity, along with an intuitive grasp of what is right or wrong in a painting, a grasp of proportion, colour, tone and composition, and above all the ability to express himself with a brush in an arresting manner. This is not to say that he had already achieved the technical mastery which increases steadily with long experience: this we shall not encounter before his Flemish period. For this reason we cannot ascribe to him prior to the characteristic works of the Dutch period, a group of 'youthful works' of inferior quality, as has sometimes been done. When would he have painted these pictures? They can be distinguished from the works ascribed to Brouwer with greater certainty by the absence of a pure colour sense, of the terse, effective typing of character, stance and gesture; they lack Brouwer's command of a situation, the plausible human reaction, and both technical and mental suppleness. In all these respects these so-called early works are coarse, empty and flaccid. Conspicuously absent is his 'wit', that innate quality which he was inclined to exaggerate rather than suppress.

A good number of these paintings are evidently the work of one painter. In the foreground there are often one or more large or medium-sized jars with a small opening. This 'Painter of the Large Jars' draws his figures on a bigger scale than does Brouwer, in a broad, sketchy manner; the heads look as if they were carved from wood; the flat strokes with which the

5. 'PAINTER OF THE LARGE JARS', SEVEN MEN CAROUSING
City Art Gallery, Bristol

6. UNIDENTIFIED PAINTER, SCHOOL INTERIOR
Courtesy of the John G. Johnson Art Collection, Philadelphia

wooden bodies are slapped onto the canvas put one in mind of house-painter's work; the faces, treated according to a fixed scheme, reduced to a few rigorously conceived types with large, generally open mouths; they are more or less humorous, which is certainly not typical of Brouwer, and not incorrectly drawn, but the artist repeats himself within a small circle of ex-
2 pressions and motifs; the settings are also broadly handled, but are composed of a few distinctive elements; the treatment of space is generalized. This scheme of recurring details and
3 types does not fit our idea of Brouwer's nature. The light is flat and of the same quality throughout. Why are these paintings ascribed to Brouwer? From the reproductions in the Rijks-
4 bureau voor Kunsthistorische Documentatie I have been able to put together eleven pictures which appear to be the work of this painter, and have observed a line of development; this fact
5 in itself rules out an attribution to Brouwer, for, if they show a development, they cannot be the work of an extremely short beginning period. The most wooden in treatment—and in these the jars are most conspicuous—appear to be the earliest and also the least comparable to Brouwer's work. A few with more skilful, more intricate compositions have a closer connection to some details of a genuine Brouwer such as the background group of the Pancake Woman
37 in the Johnson Collection in Philadelphia. The scenes in the backgrounds of paintings by this Painter of the Large Jars are inconceivable without assuming that Brouwer's work furnished the precedent; and yet the painting shows a spirit and execution entirely different from Brouwer's. The figures are somewhat caricature-like, coarse and sketchy imitations of Brouwer's own acutely characterized (yet none the less convincing), pithy and witty figures. The colours and tonalities suggest that these paintings originated in the early 1630's (which again rules Brouwer out) in the neighbourhood of Frans Hals and of such painters as Molenaer and Judith Leyster. It is noteworthy that one of these paintings came to the Rijksmuseum in Amsterdam when Schmidt-Degener was Director of it. A gift from the art dealer Goudstikker, it entered the collection as a 'Buytewegh' and was subsequently re-named a 'Brouwer'. (It has not been on exhibit since the war.)[1]
6   Then there are some scenes with school children (Bode 8 and 9)[2] and those depicting characters with 'bird-beak faces' (Bode 11 and 20). The painter of the latter appears to be identical with the painter of compositions in which a woman (or less often a man) in a
10 conspicuous white apron sits in the right or left foreground (Bode 10 and 11). A group of people is gathered round a table, seated so that a place in the centre foreground is left open. These appear to form a group of early canvases by this painter; they are more brightly coloured and less dependent on tone than his later works (such as Bode 20), more directly plastic and in general tamer. In these later works the 'bird-beak' type comes to predominate,

[1] This painter is considered further in Appendix A, where a list of his paintings is given.
[2] These numbers refer to the illustrations in Bode's work.

7. UNIDENTIFIED PAINTER, TAVERN SCENE
Art Dealer Duits, London

8. UNIDENTIFIED PAINTER, TAVERN SCENE
Coll. K. Beindorff, Hanover

9. UNIDENTIFIED PAINTER, FIGHT
Formerly Coll. Count Kersenbrock, Berlin-Grünewald

10. UNIDENTIFIED PAINTER, SCHOOL INTERIOR
Staatliche Museen, Berlin-Dahlem

11. Unidentified Painter
Lame Musician
Formerly Art Dealer D. Vaarties, Rotterdam

12. Unidentified Painter
Organ Grinder
Coll. Louwman, Wassenaar (Holland)

7 and the painting is broad, sketchy and fluid. The fact that Bode can compare these paintings with those of Hals' younger sons argues against dating them in the very beginning of Brouwer's
8 career, when those sons were still in the cradle. Moreover, the fact that one can distinguish an evolution involving distinct changes which could only have taken place over a number of
9 years, excludes Brouwer's authorship.

Another more or less clear-cut group of paintings which have been incorrectly regarded as early Brouwers are the outdoor genre scenes with many small figures in a village square, preferably near an inn. This is a Flemish-Dutch type developed from the original example of Pieter Bruegel the Elder by such diverse painters as Vinckboons, Esaias van de Velde or Drooghsloot. Günther Böhmer, in his study 'Der Landschafter Adriaen Brouwer' (Munich, 1940) has brought together a number of these works. Although he rejects many Brouwer attributions, he still appears to be too uncritical, in imagining that the hallmark of an early work is clumsiness and poor drawing.

There is one painting of this type which is certainly by Brouwer, from the end of his Dutch
40 period: the Fight over Cards in the Mauritshuis. The execution is magnificent, the painter's imprint is pungent, the treatment of landscape is fresh and lively and full of imagination, and the psychological element is treated with acrid keenness—not so much humour as relentless naturalism. The entire painting, in short, is in the typical Brouwer manner, and once more excludes the possibility that the twenty-four-year-old painter had previously gone through a
12 stage of painting such inept, empty canvases as those just considered. It is consequently

34

13. Unidentified Painter, Quacksalver
Staatliche Kunsthalle, Karlsruhe

unnecessary to demonstrate the absurdity of ascribing to Brouwer works as the Organ Grinder (Bode 7),[1] the Quacksalver (Galerie Karlsruhe, Bode 24, Böhmer 6), the Lame Musician (Böhmer 2), a Hog-Slaughtering (ibid. 3), Farmers near a Butcher's Tent (ibid. 12). They are too wooden and empty, too insipid and clumsy. Böhmer himself puts question marks to his numbers 33 (a Hurdy-gurdy Man by the Door of a House), 34 (a Fishmarket) and 36 (a Quacksalver). The figures in these are relatively large and the surroundings are only roughly indicated, in contrast to similar compositions which deserve to be considered as Brouwer's. Böhmer 2, 3 and 13 might be by the same hand; whose this might be is beyond my knowledge (and interest).

(¹) There are at least three versions of this composition known, one of which has some bare trees before the house-fronts. (Böhmer's 1 seems to be the same painting as Bode's 7 after cleaning.) In Bode's later publication of 1928 in the 'Reportorium für Kunstwissenschaft' he announced that one of these compositions bears the 'genuine' signature 'Brouwer 1621' on the sign board (Brouwer was then sixteen!)

A few compositions with figures on this scale and with kindred subjects can be referred back to models by Brouwer: such is Peasants Dancing in the collection of S. van den Bergh, Wassenaar, Holland (Bode 23, Böhmer 12), formerly in the Schloss Collection in Paris; there exists also a second version of this, which is crude and hard like the Quacksalver, already mentioned.

There is this group of open-air paintings which depict, in a more or less burlesque fashion, the life of a country village: some have small-scale figures, others large; and the quality is most uneven. They are possibly connected with Haarlem, that is to say with Frans Hals' studio, but nothing is known with certainty. Because Brouwer worked there and derived his motifs from the same circles, these pictures have been regarded either as his or as having some connection with him. It is likely that other painters worked in this vein. (One should avoid using the word 'master' for the numerous seventeenth-century bunglers who tried to meet the enormous demand on the part of the Dutch of that day for humorous pictures: their work has little or nothing to do with art.) A few types such as the Hurdy-gurdy Man (Bode 7) suggest some re-
40 lationship with the Hals entourage. But the *Fight over Cards* in the Mauritshuis is so far superior to the other paintings, which repeat and vary a limited number of motifs, that it demonstrates the impossibility of regarding Brouwer as the author of the others. Above all the spirit of this grim, serious work, with its fierce psychological penetration of the people involved in the knife fighting, and especially the superb representation of the standing ruffian, is entirely different from the spirit of the other, purely illustrative canvases—a spirit which manifests the somewhat condescending attitude of the city-dweller toward country life. The Skittle Players, of which several very dissimilar versions are known (among others Böhmer 10), belongs to this
14 group, as do the two village scenes with a man in the foreground lying stretched out face down on a bench (Museum Antwerp, Böhmer 7), and also the painting with the pair of lovers
15 on a bench by a tree and a man in a typical lansquenet costume (Böhmer 8). This last is certainly better than the others, but still that is no reason to attribute it to Brouwer. It looks Flemish. An ever-recurring peculiarity of these landscapes filled with small, detailed elements is that they move from left to right: in the left foreground one or more people are entering the picture, whereas the right foreground remains empty. The construction of the perspective follows the same tendency. Imitations, repetitions and variations of these compositions occur repeatedly, but none of them is of a quality to justify regarding it as a Brouwer. (We shall return to these problems when dealing with Brouwer's works separately.)

There are, then, only a few paintings left which can be regarded with certainty as the work of Brouwer's Dutch years. They already bear the stamp of great artistry rather than of youthful inexperience; they are already masterpieces, but are distinguished from later creations by a certain youthful tendency to overemphasize character traits, and by a less subtle realization

14. Unidentified Painter, Village Scene
Koninklijk Museum voor Schone Kunsten, Antwerp

15. Unidentified Painter, Village Scene
Coll. G. E. Bührle, Zürich

of the nature of matter and of light. But they are not awkward or empty or misdrawn; they do not lack either imagination or spirit. Above all they testify to Brouwer's great craftsmanship and to the love and devotion with which he worked; they reflect his pleasure in bold and trenchant images and in delicate nuances of tone and colour.

There is also much chaff among the wheat as regards the works ascribed to Brouwer's Antwerp period; but different factors come into play. Here we are concerned with copies, imitations and fakes—with works which were produced to pass as 'Brouwers'. Also from this period are works of others rashly ascribed to him—chiefly because of the high market value of his slender output.

The earliest records after his arrival in Antwerp show that he was already well known when he came, not only as a painter of arresting and singular canvases with farmers and soldiers in their pot-houses, but also as a refined and accomplished artist. Only in this case would Rubens have had him expressly state that a Brouwer in his possession was the only one that he had done of that subject; and only in this case would Rubens have collected as many of his rare paintings as he could lay his hands on, in spite of the fact that Brouwer's painting was so unlike his own. The essential values of Brouwer's art were indeed quite well recognized in his own time. Copies of his work must have appeared at once, copies which came so close to the originals, even in imitating Brouwer's strong points, that a fellow-painter would be uncertain. Or did Brouwer in fact repeat himself? This was not, in itself, exceptional in the seventeenth century, particularly with artists who kept a studio as a sort of business concern. Rubens admitted as much about his own work: he conducted a business like this with journeymen copyists, and, since the great master's way of painting could be translated into a formula, a deceptive similarity could be achieved. But is a really identical copy by the artist's own hand to be expected from Brouwer, considering the way he worked? Can one imagine Brouwer copying in every particular a finished canvas conceived and executed with the greatest sensitivity, and dominated by a painting technique both spontaneous and artistic; would he have been careful not to change a single jar among the still-life accessories, or not to remove a single curl or straw? A true artist never sees his own work as so definitive and absolute that it cannot be improved. Might the commission have specified a copy? Would a collector have wanted him to duplicate another painting exactly, and would Brouwer have done it if asked? The point is that there exist almost identical copies of several compositions. Reason urges one to deny that he was responsible for such repetitions. In making comparisons one must let the master's 'handwriting', with its spontaneity of expression, speak for itself. In the case that only a copy remains, how is one to recognize it as such? Only by means of an acute 'graphological' grasp of Brouwer's artistic handwriting.

In the imitations either of whole compositions or of parts which are so crude that there can be

38

no doubt that they are copies, the emphasis has shifted from the sharp analysis of human reactions to the anecdote. (From the prevalence of such paintings one can judge how much Brouwer's reputation rested on the character of his subjects—and even they were misunderstood.) They are, therefore, not the work of apprentices or journeymen. Did Brouwer indeed have a workshop for such people? We know only that d'Andois was entered as an apprentice in 1632. (Except for the fact that he became a master in 1637, he is otherwise unknown.) Brouwer also gave advice and help to Joos van Craesbeeck, who was Brouwer's age but had turned from baking to painting only late in life.

JOOS VAN CRAESBEECK

Craesbeeck is no imitator, although he borrows much from Brouwer's example. He goes his own way. He gives no evidence of Brouwer's conspicuous devotion to the noble and beautiful craft of painting, or of any feeling for fine nuances. He does not imitate the essence of Brouwer's art. His accents are gross, but he has acquired the skill to produce competent paintings as well as awkward, more or less anecdotal, and often unpleasant pictures. But such a canvas as the beautiful *Painter's Studio* in the Louvre, which portrays a distinguished patron coming to pose 16 with his small retenue, far exceeds Craesbeeck's powers and spirit—while it is not quite good 17 enough to be by Brouwer himself, whose hand the perceptive Bürger Thoré thought he 18 recognized here. A warm totality prevails which puts one in mind of Brouwer, but it lacks his mysterious, half-revealing chiaroscuro, and surely Brouwer would not have depicted the dignified elegance of the party without irony. The approach and the actual style of painting is fluid and pictorial in contrast to Craesbeeck's hard, blunt manner, and to his flatly stated, concrete figures. The matter-of-factness so typical of Craesbeeck even in those ghostly scenes where bewreathed skeletons dance is conspicuously absent here. The drawing and the brushwork as well as the characterization are more precise and more imaginative than in the latter's work. The painter's touch, particularly in the faces, is astonishing. Each face both suggests a personality and plays a part in the drama depicted; the artist's handwriting changes constantly as required. Especially masterful are the two main figures, of the painter and his pompous but jovial model, the latter graciously willing to accommodate himself to the artist's surroundings. The arrangement of a few lively colour accents against the black and warm brown of the costumes brings to mind Terborgh: the beautiful deep burgundy-red of the table-cloth and chair upholstery, the orange-red sleeve of the man at the right, the carmine bow on the painter's coat. Could Craesbeeck have so surpassed himself? Has Brouwer lent a hand? Or was the immediate influence of his personality so strong (as was Rembrandt's

16. UNIDENTIFIED PAINTER, PAINTER'S STUDIO
Musée du Louvre, Paris

influence on his pupils, if only temporarily)? The known, sometimes monogrammed work of the erstwhile baker is, to judge from the costumes, from later years; and is incomparably less imposing, of a more bourgeois, insipid spirit. Is there really any reason to ascribe this painting to Craesbeeck in spite of its great dissimilarity to his other work, except for the fact that he was Brouwer's only well-known pupil? On the analogy of this unfounded attribution, other works which are not good enough for Brouwer, but have some sort of connection with him, have been given to Craesbeeck.

These attributions may be based on the assumption of too close a relationship between Craesbeeck and Brouwer. If Brouwer was already lodging with du Pont on April the twenty-sixth, 1634, he could have stayed with Craesbeeck only a couple of months after his sojourn in the Citadel. Craesbeeck does not appear with Brouwer in any legal documents, as do du Pont,

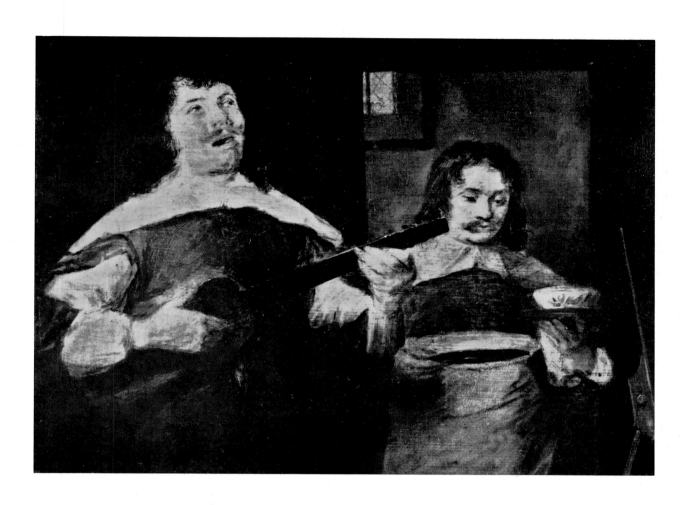

17-18. Painter's Studio (details)
Musée du Louvre, Paris

de Jode, Lievens and de Heem; these men, not Craesbeeck, were Brouwer's real friends—perhaps Craesbeeck was simply too coarse.

A characteristic work that shows him at his best is the large painting of *The Rederijkers* in the
19 Brussels Museum, which, going by the costumes, must have been painted about 1645,[1] six or
20 seven years after Brouwer's death; nonetheless it is a fairly early example of his authentic work. There is little of Brouwer's influence left, except in the landscape perspective on the right. The treatment of the figures and light, however, is almost diametrically opposed to Brouwer's. Whereas the latter's light, sensitive touch endows a face with light and spirit, the 'rederijkers'' faces are carefully and solidly modelled, built up in shades of light and dark. In some of the minor figures, where less emphasis is called for, and the artist attempts a more painterly style, he only succeeds in being heavy-handed. One of the figures in this work, the little girl sitting with the dog in the foreground, happens to be comparable to the figure of the small page on the right of the Painter's Studio in the Louvre: yet what a contrast! The page is thinly painted; he has about him a certain veiled tenderness, a shy, reflective strangeness. The girl is stiff and wooden, with hard contours, ugly, oldish features; yet she has been keenly observed. Craesbeeck appears, in a *Scene Outside an Inn* in Kassel, about 1650, still more prosaic, more positive in his modelling, and accordingly less imaginative in his style. The subject is a group of people around a table in front of an inn. A landscape view on the right with a threatening stormy sky still suggests Brouwer's influence—about twelve years after his death.

A few years ago a *Small Landscape* monogrammed by Craesbeeck came to light[2]; it shows a full moon between clouds, and has similarities with these two landscape views (in the Louvre
23 Painter's Studio and the picture in Kassel), and with a few small Brouwer landscapes, especially with the small panel in the Louvre. What in Brouwer's style is quick and spontaneous, here is superficial and sketchy and altogether harder and more mannered. Here lies a warning: this type of landscape, often attributed to Brouwer, may in fact be by Craesbeeck. The small panel
110 showing a path by a cottage in the dunes, in the Johnson Collection in Philadelphia, for example, is not up to the level of Brouwer's landscape in the Louvre. The out-of-scale couple apparently standing on a sort of sunken roadway in the middle distance argues against a Brouwer attribution. This sort of road is not a feature of a dune landscape, and certainly not in front of a cottage.

The Rederijkers, in Brussels, and the Scene Outside an Inn, in Kassel, are sound representations of reality, strongly modelled in light and dark—the dark a little too black. They have quite
21 good characterization without exaggeration, technically accountable drawing, and landscapes
22 perspectives which are more related to Brouwer's example than any other feature. In these respects Craesbeeck's best qualities appear here; he seems to have exerted himself in these

[1] Prof. F. W. S. van Thienen has been kind enough to confirm this.
[2] Mrs. F. C. Legrand of Brussels kindly called my attention to this painting.

42

19. Joos van Craesbeeck, The 'Rederijkers'
Koninklijk Museum voor Schone Kunsten, Brussels

20. Joos van Craesbeeck, The 'Rederijkers' (detail)
Koninklijk Museum voor Schone Kunsten, Brussels

43

works, in connection with the portraits in them, which were probably commissioned. They also show that Craesbeeck's later development paralleled the general course of painting within the Netherlands—and outside as well—, turning away from sharp contrasts of light and dark for the sake of a flat, even lighting, which shows everything clearly. The time was past for experiments in painting, particularly in the actual 'artist's handwriting', which were so typical of the 1630's (markedly so for Brouwer). Now forms were to be rendered according to classical principles carefully and emphatically—there was no room left for the kind of painting which suggested rather than stated—a style which Rembrandt alone continued. Craesbeeck takes us back to the earlier stage, when the chiaroscuro effect as well as the delineation of forms by suggestion was still esteemed: *The Five Senses*, for example, in the Museum in Antwerp probably dates from the end of the thirties,[1] from about the time of Brouwer's death.

24 Brouwer's precedent is obvious in the couple by the fireplace in the background; the painting also shows how much, stylistically, Craesbeeck owed to his master—but with what an appalling difference in quality. In spite of the fact that both have straight hair, the little boy shows no kinship with the page in the Painter's Studio, but with the girl in The Rederijkers. In the Antwerp painting we are face to face with Craesbeeck in his Brouwer period, and the man behind the table with his mouth wide open is perhaps Craesbeeck's crude imitation and variant of the smoker in Brouwer's painting in New York.

There is still another noteworthy difference between Brouwer and Craesbeeck: the master restricts himself to the rather small and even very small format, while his disciple favours a larger scale. We find a parallel in the case of Rembrandt and Lievens in their Leiden period.

A *Tavern Fight in ' 't Wapen van Antwerpen'* gives a reliable picture of what Joos van Craesbeeck was capable of at the end of the thirties. And he was capable of a good bit: it is a complicated 25 scene with many active figures in a dazzling, raking light, contrasted against the dark areas. Its clear-cut representation of form and metallic colour scheme are evidence of a high degree of competence. The conception and execution of the scene are as foreign to Brouwer as the subject is congenial to him. Again the painting is not signed; but it can be ascribed to Craesbeeck without reservation. This is not the case with a number of other paintings belonging to Brouwer's sphere, but not good enough to be considered the work of the master himself: such is the Tavern Scene in the Frans Hals Museum in Haarlem. The reproductions of both this painting and of The Smokers in the Metropolitan Museum are in the Witt Library in London under 'Craesbeeck', although they are certainly not by the same hand. To speak of the New York Smokers as an 'exceptionally good Craesbeeck', one must leave out of account his actual ability; the judgment rests exclusively on a misinterpreted connection with Craesbeeck's

[1] Prof. van Thienen puts the costumes at this date.

44

21. JOOS VAN CRAESBEECK, SCENE OUTSIDE AN INN
Staatliche Kunstsammlungen, Kassel

22. JOOS VAN CRAESBEECK, SCENE OUTSIDE AN INN (DETAIL)
Staatliche Kunstsammlungen, Kassel

23. Joos van Craesbeeck, Small Landscape
Present whereabouts not known

24. Joos van Craesbeeck, The Five Senses
Koninklijk Museum voor Schone Kunsten, Antwerp

25. JOOS VAN CRAESBEECK, 'IN 'T WAPEN VAN ANTWERPEN'
Koninklijk Museum voor Schone Kunsten, Antwerp

26. JOOS VAN CRAESBEECK, DEATH IS QUICK AND VIOLENT
Koninklijk Museum voor Schone Kunsten, Antwerp

47

Smoker in the Louvre. Some time ago Schneider[1] pointed out that the head of the smoker in the Louvre by Craesbeeck appears to be the same as that of the man sitting in the foreground of the New York painting—but the enormous qualitative difference made it difficult for him to regard the Paris *Smoker* as a preliminary study for the other, in New York, and Winkler[2] rejected this theory entirely, pointing to yet another variant of the head in the Louvre, with a cloth tied around it and the left eye shut. The opposite seems the case: Craesbeeck took one head out of Brouwer's Smokers, in New York, enlarged and coarsened it, producing a composition, of which he subsequently painted variations.

Craesbeeck's later development is well represented by a large painting in Antwerp, to be dated, perhaps, only a few years after The Rederijkers in Brussels: *Death is Quick and Violent* is neither a beautiful nor an attractive picture, but it is clever in many details. There is a striking 26 contrast between the appallingly vulgar, flat representations of the four figures at the right, and the fierceness and almost demoniac possession of several of the fighting figures and particularly the extreme grimness of Death itself. In a few details, such as the skeleton which is emerging from the beer jug in the lower right, Craesbeeck surprises us with the fineness of his painting. The colours are warm and beautiful. The baker has become an experienced craftsman-painter, forceful, if common and coarse. Later the forcefulness will lose out to a grey, somewhat chalky tonalism—in keeping with the general development of the times—and the subjects will become more jovial, not to say sentimental.

It is an oversimplification to ascribe to Craesbeeck everything that does not come up to Brouwer' standards. The Painter's Studio, in the Louvre, is an indication that there is a third, hitherto unrecognized artist to be considered.

JAN LIEVENS

Works by two other important artists in their own right, Jan Lievens and David Teniers the Younger, have also been ascribed to Brouwer, thereby obscuring our understanding of the master. 35 The beautiful portrait of Brouwer in the Lugt Collection drawn by Lievens testifies to the personal relationship existing between the two painters, as do the various deeds. Lievens was only slightly younger than Brouwer and was a fully formed artist when he came to Antwerp from Leiden (by way of London). He was very impressionable and easily influenced, as his large Leiden works demonstrate: he took Rembrandt's motifs, ideas and compositions, enlarged them to a startling degree... and emptied them of all meaning. It is remarkable that Constantijn Huygens, in his well-known and perceptive discussion of the two young Leiden painters in his

(¹) H. Schneider in 'Festschrift Friedländer', 1927, p. 150.
(²) F. Winkler in 'Pantheon', 1936, p. 163 ff.

27. Jan Lievens, Landscape
Private Collection, formerly Leonard Koetser Coll., London

autobiography, does not appear to have grasped the true nature of the relationship between them. He noted especially the larger format of Lievens' work as opposed to Rembrandt's self-restraint, which is indeed characteristic of their contrasted temperaments. Apparently Lievens was not satisfied with this enlarging and hollowing out of Rembrandt's conceptions for, after separating from this dominating friend, he changed his tack. We wonder if he has entered into a similar relationship with Brouwer, but find only some points of contact, to which can be attributed the fact that Lievens' small landscapes were for a long time ascribed to Brouwer. Brouwer's example may have determined the general type and also the format of these works. But they are neither imitations, nor attempts to imitate. Schneider[1] had little trouble separating Lievens' small (and also a few large) landscapes from Brouwer's. These paintings, which must be reckoned among Lievens' best, have little of those qualities which distinguish Brouwer's creations as pure nature studies: delicacy, feeling for atmosphere, impressionistic fluidity. Lievens' paintings are of a heavier tone, more positive, more precise and, for all their romantic appearances, more concrete in delineating forms.

In my opinion Brouwer's influence here has been overstated: these two artists were of quite

[1] 'Jan Lievens, sein Leben und seine Werke', Haarlem 1932, p. 57 ff.

different temperaments. Schneider says that Lievens is better linked—oddly enough—with Craesbeeck, at least as regards his figure compositions. To judge, however, from Schneider's own illustration, the Miser Surprised by Death of 1638 (Schneider, Plate 138), the theory does not fare too well. Only the theme could have been inspired by Craesbeeck's picture of Death. All the grimness which gave the latter its suggestive power is wanting in Lievens' painting. What then is left? Nothing, really, but a chilling, coquettish craftsmanship.

DAVID TENIERS

David Teniers was three or four years younger than Brouwer, so he would have been about twenty when Brouwer came to Antwerp. This difference in years, at such an age, would have made him the more susceptible to the ascendancy of the painter newly arrived from Holland. He was a pupil of his father, David Teniers the Elder, to whom, in fact, all sorts of works are attributed for no good reasons, so that it is difficult to distinguish between the works of father and son. A few religious compositions, entirely unlike his other work and showing the influence of the early Rubens school, have been ascribed to the elder Teniers. With perhaps more certainty he may be held responsible for several landscapes with small figures, which indeed foreshadow the son. These were painted under the lingering influence of Elsheimer, with whom he is said to have studied in Rome. But the typical Teniers paintings, at one time so admired, are those of the son—although the father may in his later years have worked in the successful style of his son. The elder was chiefly interested in the art trade and other speculative transactions, which had landed him in prison at just about the time Brouwer came to Antwerp. His son was not yet a master. It is not likely that the ambitious young Teniers would have chosen to continue his father's 32 kind of painting, when his father was neither successful nor of a very good reputation. Brouwer was enjoying success in his genre. The young Teniers shows a marked dependence in his earlier works on the example of the newcomer; and the well-known 'Teniers genre' exhibited in these paintings thus appears to go back not to Teniers' father but to Brouwer. And this in spite of Teniers' natural tendency, for one can scarcely imagine a greater contrast than that between the refined, sharp, bitter Brouwer and the flat and bourgeois-sentimental Teniers. For almost half a century after Brouwer's death, Teniers, who lived until 1690, produced a seemingly endless series of canvases in the genre of his great predecessor. In Teniers' hands the genre declined into a type of banal idyll in which the good and humble peasant displays respect and affection for his noble landlord. The latter, often the man who has commissioned the painting, is shown with his family graciously visiting the peasant's hut, or taking an interest in the peasant's domestic pleasures and holiday celebrations. Such is the spirit of the increasingly elegant

Teniers, court painter and art curator to the Governor. He did not manage to get a title of nobility, but he was granted a coat of arms, and he married first the daughter of Jan Bruegel the Elder, and immediately after her death a rich and distinguished young woman.

He was an amazingly clever and productive painter, but often smooth, nonchalant and easy where Brouwer would have been painfully careful, conscientious and apposite. His lighting and his representation of atmosphere and material were as uniform and unimaginative as Brouwer was, in these respects, mysterious. The insincere spirit of his arcadian scenes contrasts with the ruthless honesty of Brouwer's picture of brutalized humanity.

Teniers' true nature became dominant shortly after Brouwer's death, but in his earliest period he exhibited the ability of a genuinely great artist. It is difficult to make out how much this ability was based on youthful enthusiasm, on a fire not yet extinguished, and how much it owed to the stimulus of the radically different Brouwer. One would, perhaps, hesitate, a little, to say whether Brouwer or Teniers was responsible for some of the works of these years.

Among the glut of works supposed to be by Teniers, those numerous scenes which are more or less paraphrases of similar Brouwer pictures apparently date from this time: in these works appear almost all of the figures and many of the groups featured in Brouwer's work toward the end of his life; but somewhat changed, or put in different situations, or, more to the point, deprived of their most striking and shocking characteristics. Teniers takes over the settings and constructions of Brouwer's scenes indiscriminately, but his work is drier and more prosaic; he is facile and slick whereas Brouwer is spirited, subtle, sometimes oppressive and almost always delightfully sensitive in his details. The space on one side, usually the right, recedes deeply (but in Teniers' paintings the light remains even and flat throughout). There is a half-open door, through which someone peers; a shelf with pots and pans; a few steps leading to a side door through which someone, only partly seen, is entering or leaving. Teniers changes the rather gruesome old man or filthy woman into a servant girl offering food or drink (which is much more pleasant). Distinctive of Teniers, over against Brouwer, is the uniform, cool, flat tone (which becomes steadily cooler and flatter); the midpoint of the picture is repeatedly a white head-dress or night-cap or a white shirt, such as appears once in a Brouwer, in the Arenberg- 34 Dulwich composition. There the shirt is truly the high light of the composition; with Teniers it is simply the lightest colour. Similarly distinctive of Teniers is the positive, solid, often very clever manner of painting, where neither uncertainty nor suggestion plays a part. Another feature is the long, narrow breeches which stop a bit above the ankle and make the legs look like badly stuffed sausages.

One must be cautious in discussing these paraphernalia, for Teniers apparently enjoyed no less a success with them than did Brouwer with his. Here too the distinction must be drawn between genuine and false; and much, even in the great public collections, is wrongly ascribed

51

to Teniers. It is bewildering and irritating to note how freely Teniers' name is given to works which in no respect suggest the hand of this very able painter. A sharp and systematic sifting of this work, a delimitation such as we are attempting here for Brouwer, would perhaps lead to surprising results and would certainly heighten the appreciation of his art. He was too sound a craftsman to have painted all that mediocre work; particularly among the later works are many paintings which derive from his mid- and late-seventeenth century imitators and successors, such as Ryckaert or van Herp—'successors' because it is a question of a continuing commercial production designed to satisfy the public demand. There are among these paintings direct copies after Brouwer, such as the copy of The Smokers in the Metropolitan Museum in New York, but to ascribe this inferior work to Teniers bespeaks a low estimate of him as an artist. In the Wadsworth Atheneum in Hartford, Connecticut, there is a small copy after the composition in Dulwich, marked 'Teniers' in small letters, but the authenticity of such a slack piece of work is doubtful. To make direct copies of another's work would perhaps not have been the practice of this fluent painter. Teniers was an artist whose production already enjoyed a position of its own and apparently its own market; and such copies would have compromised him.

This entire mass of work has a peculiar importance for the study of Brouwer's œuvre: not a single composition, nor a single figure from those paintings by Brouwer which I consider as Dutch, occurs in Teniers' work; which provides indirect evidence for the correctness of my division. For example, the Feast of the Cook, a notable composition from the end of the early period, known in three versions (one of which is in Boston) has left no trace in Teniers' work, however striking the rear view of the principal figure and however tempting his white jacket would have been. This justifies placing the work in the period of transition from Holland to Antwerp, before contact with Teniers.

Teniers' natural impulse to please his customers has little in common with that in Brouwer's mentality which leads him to reveal ruthlessly man's passions, baseness, his brutalization by drink and tobacco. Their apprehensions of art follow opposite directions, not only in their portrayal of man himself, but also in everything that touches the atmosphere he lives in, above all in the treatment of light. Teniers' blond, even colour and Brouwer's deep tension-laden tonality are miles apart. Teniers' painting could not have been slow: the enormous demand for his works induced him to produce much, and that quickly.

The well-known *Tavern Interior* in the Frans Hals Museum in Haarlem (Bode 123), until recently ascribed to Brouwer, is in my judgement an original Teniers, with a closer connection 28 to Brouwer—both stylistically and mentally—than the paintings just mentioned. It is a good example of his early, painstaking art. The woman on the right is a recognizable Teniers type; and similarly the colour of the standing figure in the centre, with yellow dominating, and the

28. DAVID TENIERS
TAVERN INTERIOR
Frans Hals Museum, Haarlem

29. UNIDENTIFIED PAINTER
TEMPTATION OF ST. ANTHONY
Staatliche Museen, Berlin-Dahlem

30. COPY AFTER BROUWER, QUARTET
City of York Art Gallery, on loan from the Ettlinger Collection

53

characterization and brushwork of each figure are convincingly his. The arrangement suggests The Smokers in New York; the interior looks so much like Brouwer that the attribution is scarcely to be wondered at. Here we see Teniers in the wake of the older, greater artist, which in this case has made for a style more fluid and pictorial than usual.

Teniers, in his younger years, felt impelled to paint more fantastic imaginings. Brouwer could express such feelings in the way he treated his realistic scenes, if necessary accentuating the fierceness or the nausea. Teniers, on the other hand, had to summon the help of the ghost, the fantastic and unnatural apparition, which had been a traditional motif in Flemish art since the great precedent of Jeroen Bosch. Thus originated his Temptations of St. Anthony, a subject apparently greatly to the public taste, and his wonderful and more original Witches' Sabbaths and other witch scenes, with or without a Cerberus. He must have enjoyed painting these: they may well have satisfied an urge in his otherwise hardheaded, opportunistic disposition. They are often executed with more loving care and delicacy than his frigid country scenes. Was Brouwer Teniers' example here, too?: a *Temptation of St. Anthony* by him is mentioned several times.[1]

Brouwer, with his fierce realism, presented a relentless and repelling revelation of human passions, weaknesses and degeneracy; Teniers, who wanted neither to disgust nor to hurt, sought a way of parodying society and found it in his moralizing monkey- and cat scenes. These, or at least the best among them, must be early works, because of their often surprisingly keen and vivid character portrayal, their pithy, fascinating and expressive style, and the concentrated lighting effects: in the forties, throughout the painting in both North and South Netherlands, this concentrated treatment of light was superseded by a flatter, more neutral and even tonality with more marked colour contrasts—as shown in Craesbeeck's development. Perhaps contact with Brouwer's sardonic spirit provoked Teniers to these mockeries, which were not meant to offend anybody. He could also have found these animal motifs in the work of Jan Bruegel the Elder, who became his father-in-law in 1637 and influenced him toward an entirely different—although no less Flemish—artistic direction from Brouwer's.

(1) Since Rubens owned a Temptation of St. Anthony by Brouwer, there is good evidence that Brouwer had painted the subject, although no example is known today. It also appears in an Antwerp inventory of 1652 (van den Branden, p. 37). The Staatliche Museen in Berlin ascribe a panel of 27.2 × 21 cm. with this subject to Brouwer, as, indeed, 'frühes Bild des Meisters.' I have not seen the work but, to judge from the reproduction, this ascription is astounding. Even if it were a Brouwer, it would not fit into the framework of his early work, if only because of the tone and the treatment of the background, which are entirely in accordance with the manner of Antwerp art between 1630 and 1640. But it is no Brouwer. Nowhere does the reproduction show his crisp and delicately sensitive touch; there are coarse details (in the first place, the head and hands of St. Anthony) which are unacceptable as Brouwer's work. Equally impossible for this realist are the ghostly little figures in the sky, taken over from Bosch or Bruegel. There are suggestive details, such as the Goya-like death's-head mask in the lower left corner, but these are insufficient reasons for ascribing the panel to Brouwer. Then whose is it? I do not know; certainly not Teniers', even if he dealt with this subject often.

31. Unidentified Painter, Champion Drinker

Rijksmuseum, Amsterdam

32. David Teniers, Man with Glass of Beer

Musée du Louvre, Paris

55

Is Teniers also working with a Brouwer theme in those small paintings of only the shaggy head and shoulders of a peasant in some instances looking at a glass of beer that he is holding before his eyes? There are strikingly good examples bearing Teniers' monogram. Closer inspection convinces us that not one of these heads is an original Brouwer. They are much tamer than the series of heads which we shall consider in discussing Brouwer's works; they are more fluidly pictorial, mostly with light backgrounds; but without anything of the obsessive and penetrating qualities of Adriaen's unquestionable works, so that one must conclude that Teniers himself was the creator of this genre (of which there are good examples in Dulwich College). It should be added that these typified heads with stubbly beards also appear in Teniers' larger compositions and not in Brouwer's.

But it is undeniable that Brouwer's influence on Teniers' choice of subject was great, and has thus left its mark on an entire genre in Flemish painting of the mid-seventeenth century— albeit the followers omitted everything from their prototype that was essential to it.

And yet we find works of this later, commonplace type, for which Teniers is the precursor, ascribed to Brouwer. The following is a striking example. On the advice of Bode, the Champion Drinker, a composition far too large for Brouwer, and painted in the flat blond light character-
31 istic of later painting, was bought by the well-known Berlin collector James Simon, and illustrated by Bode in his book on Brouwer (Bode 103). At the Simon auction it was acquired—this time on the advice of Schmidt-Degener—by the collector de Bruijn in Spiesz, Switzerland. (His wonderful collection was left to the Rijksmuseum in Amsterdam.) Owing to the great reputation as connoisseurs of these two experts, and to the high level of the de Bruijn Collection, no one has doubted Brouwer's authorship. Nevertheless such an attribution is out of the question: the space is too vast and empty; the rear wall is flat and even and there is a strange, unarticulated gate-like entrance; the good and jovial faces of the merry-makers have nothing to do with Brouwer's individuals. Observe how lovingly the dog is looking up at its master. It is a clever and considerable work, but has no connection with Brouwer's way of painting. Can it be a Teniers? This is more likely, but there are too many discrepancies between it and Teniers' other work. If it is not a Teniers, still it is characteristic of his mentality, in contrast to Brouwer's.

REPETITIONS, COPIES, IMITATIONS

Until now we have been treating of works weeded out of the Brouwer œuvre, works belonging to categories which have been incorrectly ascribed to him. There are in addition works which do belong to the Brouwer category in the sense that from the very beginning they were intended to pass for Brouwers—but are not by his hand. Included are imitations in his spirit as well as copies. We have already demonstrated above that repetitions by Brouwer, indentical copies, down to the minutest details, that is, of his own works, are unlikely in view of his subtlety and his variability. Still there are pairs of paintings which suggest such a repetition.

First, an example from the Dutch period. In both the Johnson Collection in Philadelphia and in the Museum in Basel there is a composition showing a *Woman making Pancakes* at a 37 fireplace in the right foreground, in a room with a large peasant family at table. The two representations are alike, but there are marked differences in execution and in the portrayal of types, differences not so much of quality as of character. They are almost of a size; the Philadelphia panel, which shows a little more of the scene on all sides, is somewhat larger. Certainly this is one of the earliest of Brouwer's known compositions. The picture in Philadelphia is rougher, somewhat more careless, but also more expressive and spontaneous. On the other hand, it does not have the unparalleled solidity and immediacy, the convincing mastery of another painting in the Johnson Collection, also of a person cooking pancakes. In this second 39 picture it is a big, coarse, strange-looking man, who occupies a much more dominant position in the composition. In immediacy, solidity, and the precision of every touch, in the play of light, and its very boldness, which always comes off, it far excells the other painting.[1] Might the version in Basel be the original of the pancake-woman composition? (It is still further from the painting with the pancake-man.) It is, to be sure, more carefully painted than the Philadelphia version, better finished, but losing thereby its expressive power. Conclusion: perhaps neither of the two pictures of a woman cooking pancakes is an original; but the one in Philadelphia still stands a chance.

To consider a single painting: Bode illustrates the *Quartet*, four peasants singing over their pipes and jugs. (Bode 2; formerly in the Kappel Collection, Berlin, now on loan to the York Museum from the Ettlinger Collection.) Subject and conception fit into the framework of 30 Brouwer's art, but the execution does not. The two types behind the table are too like caricatures. Nor are we satisfied by a close inspection of, say, the sleeves of the purple jacket of the man in the foreground, or of his badly-drawn mouth. The dull grey background is not of Brouwer quality. Still there is some connection with Brouwer. One must assume that the original of this painting has been lost, or that this is an imitation of Brouwer's style. (In this case also, Bode was probably the advisor to the Berlin collector Kappel.)

As Plate 53, the *Feast of the Cook*, Bode reproduces a painting which was formerly in the collection of H. M. Clark in London, and is now in a Berlin collection about which there is some secrecy. Bode has not looked closely at this work,[2] for he speaks of a group of three

[1] See the illustrations and discussion below in the description of Brouwer's works pp. 70, 73.

[2] Nor, in fact, at the previous painting: in his list of reproductions he calls it the Quartet, while in the text he speaks of *three* peasants.

33. ADRIAEN BROUWER, FEAST OF THE COOK [REPETITION?]
Museum of Fine Arts, Boston

peasants indistinctly represented in the background. But this group consists of a seated man, another man who stands railing at him, with a child at his side, and an older woman, who stands between them listening, ready to separate them: a typically Brouwer scene. The seat of the baby-chair lacks the essential hole. There is another version, acquired by the Museum of Fine Arts in Boston from the London art dealer Duits; a painting with an excellent pedigree, having

33 been bought in 1790 (?) by Lord Palmerston in Paris. In the Boston painting there is a hole in the baby-chair: Brouwer would not have omitted it, but it could, of course, have been painted out in the other version. One should look at the supporting post which Brouwer places, as he does so often, in the foreground. (On this post marks for keeping the score often appear.) Artistically the post serves to break the space, to divide it rhythmically into two unequal parts, and at the same time it acts as a repoussoir, emphasizing depth. Unless the reproduction is deceptive, the post in the Berlin picture is drily, superficially and smoothly painted—in strong contrast to the characteristically careful and loving treatment, even to the grain of the wood, that it receives in the other painting. Is not such a difference typical of, in the one case, the copyist who does not consider the post important, and, in the other, the artist for whom nothing is too trivial? Behind the

58

post there is a white cloth lying on the chair and the ground. Observing the folds and the mobile contours of this cloth in both paintings, one detects a similar difference: the two corners on the floor lie flat, but in the Boston picture there are tiny folds in the one on the left. In the other painting one notes particularly the absence of the cast shadow on the foot-rest of the chair. These are details which might distinguish master from copyist. All this inclines one to regard the Boston painting as the original, but this is not entirely satisfactory. There is a certain dryness and matter-of-fact meticulousness about the style of this version which does not accord with Brouwer's mentality (any more than does Bode 53). There is a third example which I know only from a poor reproduction (in the Rijksbureau voor Kunsthistorische Documentatie); at one time in the collection of S. von Schidlowsky at Leningrad, it is considerably larger (53 × 79 cm.) than the Boston painting (33 × 49 cm.), and on canvas, whereas the latter is on wood. It is noteworthy that in respect to differences in small details the Leningrad painting sometimes seems to agree more with the one in Boston and sometimes more with the one in Berlin. These data are insufficient to warrant a definite judgment on the three paintings; several points argue for the one in the Russian collection.[1]

A similar case: in the Gallery of Dulwich College, near London, there hangs a comparatively large, very typically Brouwer composition of, superficially viewed, outstanding quality, the 34 *Tobacco Inn*. It is a tavern scene with two men in the left foreground, one smoking and the other filling his pipe. (These men are from a better social circle than Brouwer's tavern types usually are; possibly one of them is meant to be a self-portrait.) On the right a man stands making water against the familiar post with score marks and with a jug hanging on it.

Bode illustrates as Plate 3 an exactly similar scene from the famous Arenberg Collection in Brussels, which we have now lost to America. He says that according to a tradition this is the work that Arenberg bought from Brouwer in the Antwerp Citadel. This subject does not fit in very well with Houbraken's description, and the story itself is improbable, but Arenberg may very well have acquired the painting from Brouwer: for this, and not the version in Dulwich, appears to be the genuine one. A comparison with Bode's poor reproduction is well-nigh impossible, but a close examination of the Dulwich panel yields astonishing results. The group by the chimney in the background seems to have about the same relationship to this group in Bode 3, as do the peasants in the background of the Berlin Feast of the Cook to those in the panel in Boston. More and more imperfections appear in the Dulwich panel, bringing it below Brouwer's level. It cannot be an original, and so must be a copy; but a copy of such high quality that one wonders if Brouwer himself was not responsible for it. This possibility, however, is disproved by the absence of the liveliness and freshness of the typical Brouwer imprint. The same drawbacks as in the painting in Boston obtain here, but to a greater degree.

[1] See below, p. 86.

34. ADRIAEN BROUWER, TOBACCO INN [REPETITION]
Dulwich College Picture Gallery, London

This does not mean that the example formerly in the Arenberg Collection is the original. The illustration in Bode does not permit of any decision; and if one copy of the quality of the painting in Dulwich could be made, it could be done a second time, as appears to have been the case with the Feast of the Cook. There are still more copies of this picture known, both of the whole composition (there is one, much weaker, in the Museum at Valenciennes) and of details.

Who made such a precise copy? The extraordinary similarity between the paintings in Boston and Berlin on the one hand, and that between the Dulwich and Arenberg ones on the other, suggests that one copyist was responsible for all four. Did this copyist stand in some sort of subservient position to Brouwer, so that it would have been possible to order a precise repetition of a work by the master, an arrangement by which Brouwer might share in the profit? To judge from the working conditions in Rubens'[1] studio, such a procedure was perfectly aboveboard. (Without such a studio industry, how could portrait painters have

(1) And equally in van Dyck's.

60

filled contracts for a dozen copies of the same portrait?) The fact that Brouwer had to make a statement for Rubens that he had painted a composition only once, points to something of this sort. If this is correct, such 'second examples' are more than copies: they are repetitions produced by another hand under the master's eye, and have been more or less 'guaranteed' by him—if not, indeed, touched up. The terms 'autograph' and 'not-autograph' are therefore more accurate than 'original' and 'copy'.

This distinction, however, holds good only for the very best examples, where an inferiority to 'autograph' work appears only after very close inspection of purely technical qualities; it does not go for the numerous clumsy copies, flimsy variants and imitations that are also attributed to Brouwer. The name 'Brouwer' had become a label to be stuck onto any raw, ribald, and scabrous scene of common people (peasants, sailors, soldiers, vagrants and addicts to drink and tobacco), if the scene is presented more crudely and drastically than Teniers would have done.[1]

Only a few cases of works wrongly ascribed to Brouwer have been discussed above, not even all those which I could not help noticing in the publications of Bode and Böhmer, to say nothing of those in Schmidt-Degener's 'youthful indiscretion'. The examples I have chosen serve to illustrate certain categories of paintings which have been erroneously given to the master. In the course of the past few years many false attributions have been recognized as such. Thus the Host and his Wife in the Munich Pinakothek (Bode 115) and the Landscape in Hamburg (Bode 124) are no longer regarded by the Directors of those museums as Brouwers; nor is the Tavern Interior in Haarlem (Bode 123), ascribed above to Teniers.[2]

With this general, fundamental purification of Brouwer attributions draughted, the way is clear to take up his artistry in terms of reliable works.

[1] To mention a single instance: in the famous and select collection of Lord Ellesmere (Bridgewater Gallery) there is an exceptionally crude group of singing peasants, which clearly goes back to an original Brouwer in the type of representation and characterization; but it has nothing to do with the master in spirit or in execution. None the less, it has been accepted in the Brouwer literature, and was reproduced among the illustrations of this collection. The two paintings in the Prado are equally unoriginal, being obvious variants on well-known Brouwer compositions—one is based on the Dulwich picture. See p. 115.

[2] Above, p. 52.

PART II

35. JAN LIEVENS, PORTRAIT OF ADRIAEN BROUWER
Coll. F. Lugt, Paris

THE WORK

1. BROUWER AND HALS

In the same way that Vincent van Gogh's 'The Potato Eaters' sums up what he had been seeking in his Dutch years, Brouwer's *Peasants' Feast* (Bode 16; 35×53 cm; Ruzicka Collection, Zurich) represents what the latter had been working towards in his Dutch years. Both pictures conclude a period in the development of their creators. Their significance is this: that the painting which preceded them led, of necessity, as it were, up to these two masterpieces, and that through them an enormous tension was discharged. (Rembrandt's Night Watch fulfils the same function in his creative life: after it comes an equilibrium, a calm which introduces sounder, more disciplined, more muted works.) The analogy between van Gogh and Brouwer does not stop here. Not only are the subjects closely related; there is also a similarity in the heavy, dark tone of the paintings, and even in the peculiar relationship of the artists towards the figures depicted. Van Gogh puts himself, in this picture, in opposition to the idyllized, urban portrayal of the rustic, and attempts to penetrate to the essence of his subjects, to their very thoughts and feelings. Similarly Brouwer's Peasants' Feast stands in sharp contrast to the conception of the peasant as an object of light mockery and curiosity prevalent among the painters of peasant-life in his day. Brouwer replaces this attitude with a sardonic verism that sidesteps nothing; his drollery is not at the expense of his characters; his types and situations are as close to life as possible.

The party includes seven men, four women and a small child. One of the men has already had his fill; he is leaning out across the lower half of the door. Through the open upper half one sees the suggestion of a quiet evening landscape. Brouwer has grouped the other figures in a masterfully loose way, as naturally and unconstrainedly as possible. Each figure serves a separate function in this composition, so full of diversity; yet each figure is also a clearly marked type. The brutal face of the small fellow who peers over the edge of the table is sharply typed with a few touches of light, without losing its individual character. The company divides into two distinct groups. The one on the left forms a closed composition by itself and could be a complete painting by Brouwer. On the right is the farmer's wife—in a more muted light—, recognizable as the mistress of the house by virtue of her folded white bonnet; her whole bearing marks her as being of higher rank than the three servant-women in the other group. Her white apron is spread across her ample lap. A wonderful drunk gentleman is apparently trying to pull her onto his knees; she submits passively, with feeble resistance, as if to something inevit-

65

36. Peasants' Feast (detail, actual size)
Ruzicka Stiftung, Kunsthaus, Zürich

able. His richer, darker clothing trimmed with fur, the abundant head of hair crowning his dissolute face, and particularly his large blue hat, lying on a basket nearby, distinguish him as a man from the city—or perhaps he is the landlord. Next to her stands her fat little son, who greedily reaches for the bowl of porridge which is sliding off her lap. The rest of the company is not concerned with this scene. On the contrary: the farmer himself, in the big tub-chair, his back towards his wife, is singing with the farm hands and maidservants. The colour of the picture is almost entirely concentrated in his figure. His brick-red beret, yellow chamois jacket, moss-green sleeve, and especially the striking white of his breeches provide the strongest colour accents, brought forward by proximity to the worn, grey-brown wood and the more mauve-tinted staves of the cask. He is balanced by the fiddler on the left, who continues the colour scheme on a

66

more subdued note: pale purple breeches, steel-blue jacket, and dirty yellow cap. These two men are turned toward each other, and, with their outstretched legs, form a strong 'V' shape, framing the rest of the group and making this part of the picture an independent composition. The old woman in the black bonnet next to the farmer eagerly reaches out a pewter mug to be filled from the brown earthen beer jug held high by another woman. The liquor will shortly disappear into her large, greedily opened mouth. The other woman grins as she pours the drink. Between these two sits a young man singing with abandon to the tune of the fiddler; his arms are raised, and in one hand he holds a half-empty glass of beer. The face of a man singing boisterously appears just over the farmer's right shoulder. On the far left is another woman, also holding up a beer glass, her face full of fun. She is partly merged into the subdued background of grey wall and planking.

All this is painted with an incisive, emphatic brush, setting outlines, folds and furrows off against light areas, but with a suppleness sufficient to avoid any hardness. All the forms in their curves and convolutions are rendered with full plasticity, but the artist has also enlivened the scene with sharp, concentrated flashes, like the white pipe on the hat of the man with raised arms, and other such glancing lights. In places he shades by means of short, light brushstrokes on a dark surface, or with dark on light. Note how the white and the purple breeches-legs in the foreground have been painted; and still one can follow the black thread with which a patch has been put in the white breeches-leg.

That Brouwer was a first-rate still life painter appears from the haphazard collection of pottery utensils, frying pan, basket and firewood in the right foreground—also from the dishes and food on the table—bread, butter, a bowl of turnips, an earthenware warmer.

All Brouwer's fine qualities are already fully realized here: in the first place, the masterly way in which he has built up the group, arranging and differentiating its members; his human sympathy with the different types, and keen understanding of them; his skill in composing the scene out of different values of tone and colour, of volume and drawing; but no less the unheard-of variety of techniques at his command, ranging from the broad, free, suggestive touch, to the extremely fine, concentrated, perceptive painting of details. Each of these qualities and achievements was to prove potential of further development, and underlying relationships between them were to be subtly modified. But already he has shown himself in each respect to be a master who is entirely free to use his abilities in the service of his insights—and it is above all these insights that will change over the years.

Brouwer must have painted this picture, based primarily on the contrast of light and dark, but which does not make a colourful impression, between 1625 and 1630. It was certainly painted when he was still in Holland, and it would not be the last work from the period the painter spent in Amsterdam and Haarlem. At this time Dutch painting is emphatically based on colour, but the domination of local colour is already past. ('Local colour' is a colourful element, especially in the clothing, which is emphasized according to its own value, and not modified according to its chiaroscuro relationships. Considerations of local colour obtain in the painting done between 1610 and 1620.) In this connection one thinks of such painters as Buytewegh, Dirk Hals, Arend Arendsz., van de Venne, of the early paintings of van Goyen, and above all of Frans Hals—without even leaving the Haarlem milieu in which Brouwer's painting probably originated. Colour is being toned down. One can follow the change in the sequence of Frans Hals' paintings of the Civic Guard Companies. Consider the difference between the group-portraits of St. Adriaen's Company (Cluveniers Doelen) and St. George's Company; both dated 1627, although the first is thought—correctly—to be somewhat earlier. As did Brouwer in the Peasants' Feast, Hals has painted the St. George Company against a grey, almost even background, but—which is essential—the background is of a much lighter, more neutral tone, setting off the colour effects (yellow-orange, light blue, and salient white) in the figure group. Brouwer's darker background becomes more of an atmosphere, a dim obscurity from which colours and figures emerge ever more clearly. In this Brouwer shows a greater affinity with his contemporary Rembrandt than with his teacher Hals. Since Brouwer cannot have known of Rembrandt at this time, and Rembrandt, not quite so precocious as Brouwer, would hardly have been concerned with these problems, Brouwer was probably the more advanced of the two in the atmospheric handling of space.

The connection may be closer than one would at first suspect between Brouwer's paintings and these Hals compositions, most remarkably so with Hals' first Civic Guard picture, that of 1616: there is a truly arresting agreement in composition between the left-hand group in the Brouwer, and the Hals. This is the more noteworthy when one considers that Brouwer was completely free in grouping his figures and in rendering them more or less exactly, as he saw fit, while Hals was obliged to give equal emphasis, as portraits, to all his figures. Brouwer's farmer occupies a place as important as that of Hals' centre officer in the foreground; and Hals' figure on the extreme left may have been the precursor of Brouwer's fiddler. Even the woman behind the latter might be compared with the third figure from the right in Hals' picture: standing above the group, they fulfil like functions. Hals had painted this work years before Brouwer was apprenticed to him, and he probably did not finish another until after Brouwer had left. We may safely conjecture that Hals would have brought this major work, then displayed in the Civic Guard chamber, to his pupil's attention. It probably made a deep impression on Brouwer, who was to use it as a starting point, as a statement of the problems which he attacked in his later pictures.

Hals' picture, however, offered Brouwer no help regarding the problem of the relationship between colour and tone. The general impression of the Hals group portrait of 1616 is one of a

I. Peasants' Feast
Ruzicka Stiftung, Kunsthaus, Zürich

37. PANCAKE WOMAN
Courtesy of the John G. Johnson Collection, Philadelphia

blacker, deeper tone: but this is, in fact, not a matter of 'tone', of, that is, the relations of light and dark, but often of the inter-relations between the colours themselves. For Hals uses black as a colour here, in accordance with the above-mentioned polychrome conception of colour prevalent between 1610 and 1620; also the black of a costume serves as local colour. Between this first Guard portrait, with its brilliant, deep black against the sparkling, bluish white of the collars and cuffs, and the colourful sashes, and the Company of St. George of 1627, one can perceive Hals' search for tonalist effects. Brouwer goes a step further. Hals suppressed strong contrasts in favour of an equality of tone and colour; Brouwer, on the other hand, was clearly striving for an expression of interior atmosphere which would act as a cohesive element—and he succeeded magnificently. The representation recedes step by step into the twilight tone of the background: the standing woman on the left and the raised hands of the man in the centre lead into the still life of crockery on the shelf against the wall, painted in a deep tone; and this same tone finds

69

its completion in the man in dark-blue breeches and dull brown jacket leaning out across the lower door. The farmer's conspicuously depicted face and his glaring red cap are pushed forward by the dark-grey rear wall.

The fiddler in this painting seems to have been the exemplar for that unknown (and scarcely interesting) painter whom heretofore I have called 'the painter of the large jars'. For the latter the fiddler becomes an almost unchangeable type; moreover, this is the only painting by Brouwer in which the earthenware crockery, so important to the imitator, appears in excess. This raises the question of whether these pictures might be the work, not of a follower, but of Brouwer, during the period in which he was readying himself to paint this conclusive composition. But they are really too poor, lacking all those other qualities we have found in the great picture. The transition would have been too great, particularly when considering the fact that the painter of the Peasants' Feast would have been scarcely twenty-two. None the less there are a few compositions by Brouwer which must have been painted before the Peasants' Feast; they too bear evidence of a great mastership, and, lacking the frailties of the large-jar man's work, show that Brouwer's earliest work was along different lines from the paintings ascribed here to the follower. These early Brouwers are the Pancake Woman and the Pancake Man, both in the Johnson Collection in Philadelphia.[1]

37   One might conceive of the *Pancake Woman* as a first version of the Peasants' Feast. Here, also, a meal is the subject; but everything is much more deliberate, artificial, exaggerated in expression. The painter is out to be amusing, perhaps even to jibe—as he would never do in later life. This sort of mockery fits into the Hals environment, however: Hals himself, in the early twenties when Brouwer would have been working with him, was painting his genre scenes in a vein of wit, perhaps of irony, but always of good humour. Esaias van de Velde also has a place in this circle, but one thinks particularly of Willem Buytewegh with his elusive but pointed and refined irony. If there is some connection between Hals and Buytewegh on the one side, and Brouwer on the other, the fact remains that their social provinces and their frames of mind and intentions were completely different. Hals—consider his beautiful Merry

38 Company in New York—often takes his motifs and types from the theatre, an unreal world; and Buytewegh does so even more often, or else he creates figures so typically and gracefully stylized that they have no ties with sober, day-to-day happenings. The genre-world of Hals and Buytewegh was given its poetic expression by Bredero. Brouwer does nothing of this sort; he dramatizes hardly at all, he states flatly, in the manner of a naturalist born before his time. And his perception is not amusing or convivial or charming, like Frans Hals' in his pictures of childrens' heads; it is sharp, relentless and acid; he seems possessed by a keen

[1] The relationship of the Johnson Collection Pancake Woman to another version of the same composition in the Basel Museum has been discussed in the preceding chapter (p. 57).

38. FRANS HALS, MERRY COMPANY

Metropolitan Museum of Art, New York, Bequest of Benjamin Altman, 1913

71

interest in his fellow men, above all in those who live beyond the pale of civilization and society, the wanderer, the outcast, the good-for-nothing and the libertine. His attention also turns to the peasant, who, more than the city dweller, must look out for himself, to the farm hands and servant-women on their often barren farms. Did this reflect a romantic longing for closer contact with basic things, for a return to nature? The country people, as Brouwer depicted them, responded more directly, freely and violently to their needs and desires. Surely Brouwer was not motivated by modern social concern. Himself a libertine, as his life-story shows, he found here a kind of man who was freer, more natural, than Brouwer's fellow city-dwellers; here were people who gave themselves over without restraint to their natural passions, as did also his fishermen, soldiers, tramps and vagrants. He chose these men as his models because he found them 'picturesque', and they were picturesque because, just as their outward appearances were not determined by what was thought fashionable but by circumstance and caprice, and were consequently individual, in the same way were their very personalities, unconstrained by etiquette, openly expressed. Brouwer was fascinated by the man who lets himself go, whose inner being is exposed, whose reactions are direct and natural. For this reason he seized upon the subjects, then popular, of the five senses and the seven deadly sins. For this reason he painted men suffering torments in their heads, teeth, backs or feet under the surgeon's hands; and he was fascinated by the tense concentration of the surgeon himself, and the anxiety with which the surgeon's wife or assistant follows the operation. None of this, however, has anything of the joking spirit we have noted in the Pancake Woman.

The exuberance of youth and the desire to mock, soon to be conquered by the serious artist, still appear here. To these qualities are joined a lack of refinement and of technical skill in the execution of his craft. Yet we find elements already present which recur in his last compositions. During his short life his outlook gradually and steadily deepened, but he underwent no great inner change. In the Pancake Woman, for example, we already observe that construction in which one half (here, as generally, the right half) is much deeper than the other; a man is leaning out through the upper half of a door, and his wife and child watch him give back what he has taken too abundantly (a subject that will recur); beyond him, in a contrasting tone, is a softly-lit landscape view. Yet his earliest known picture is a far cry from the point that the artist will finally reach—after a career no longer than the fifteen years between 1622, when he is scarcely sixteen, and 1637, when he would die. Here he has chosen an exceptional figure as his chief motif, the pancake woman; later he will not require such an extravagant subject to captivate the beholder's attention. The old crone, with hunched back and long nose, sits with her back to the company round the table, to which she does not belong; in fact, she appears to be the object of the farmer's insults.

Everything here is rougher, blunter, more primitive than in the great Peasants' Feast. The people, as well as the furniture, are heavier, clumsier and shabbier; they have short and rough grey bodies, with too large heads; on the right such a ruffian is taking an old woman by the shoulder and chin; the man next to him is picking his teeth; then a laughing woman who appears to be hugging a wine glass lovingly; on the extreme left two men are having a discussion—the one in front might be a city man; in front of them sits the caricature-like, scarecrow figure of the angry farmer, near whose chair stands a small boy.

In this picture Brouwer is still a long way from the level of the Peasants' Feast. The crudeness and awkwardness, the cramped space and lack of atmosphere are all evidence of inexperience and of uncomplicated thinking. These youthful characteristics are also to be observed in the overdrawn decrepitude of the ladder leaning against the wall, or in the exaggerated grimace of the angry peasant. The pancake woman is leering at the latter with inner amusement. Her expression is wonderful. In the background behind her is that familiar doorway, the upper half opening onto a sketchy view of a wood which Brouwer has indicated schematically, with a black tree trunk in front.[1]

The pancake woman is an old witch in rags, with a crafty smile spread over her large mouth; the few teeth left in her lower jaw shine against her upper lip. She sits on a foot-stove, bent over toward the fire, with her enormous back to the eight people who are feasting; she belongs to the motley crew of vagrants who scrape together their necessities in all sorts of ways. The travelling pancake maker's seems to have been a profession in those times; there is one in a small drawing by Rembrandt in the Print Cabinet of the Rijksmuseum in Amsterdam: a boy standing in front of her appears to be fishing some money out of his deep trouser pockets to pay her with, and there is this beautiful text: 'Hael ayeren hael op dat ic een Panckoekster mach crijghen aen boort. Of eender die daer rechtevoort struyf wilde backen. En diese by dozynen onbesiens in de pan wou smacken.'[2]

Men also followed this occupation: such a one is the principal figure in the other panel in this same Johnson Collection: the *Pancake Man* (Bode 22; 33.7 × 28.2). Here Brouwer has followed his bent more exuberantly, in providing the scene with a fantastic figure. An unsavoury specimen, this cook. But that did not matter. Are there some drops hanging from his monstrous, hairy nose? He has not seen a barber for some time, nor did any tailor have a say in fashioning his wide, shapeless coat; pieces of string hold his leggings together . . . There does not seem to have been

[1] In the preceding chapter the argument was that both the Pancake Woman in Philadelphia and the one in Basel might well be copies of an original since lost: this might partly explain the defects, but naturally not altogether, as is not to be expected.

[2] 'Fetch eggs, and bring on board a pancake woman who can make a batter and slap the pancakes on the griddle by the dozen.' Quoted in the 'Woordenboek der Nederlandse Taal' under 'pannekoeken' as the words of Mr. Kackadoris in 'Een tafelspel van Meester Kackadoris ende een Doof-Wijf met Ayeren', Amsterdam, n.d. 1596.

much money in his job. Next to him sits his lumpy, shapeless wife, huddled over the glowing fire in sleepy comfort—like the pudgy house cat that appears in other Brouwer pictures.

Placed in the middle of the composition, this man has become its real motif. Brouwer has treated him monumentally, drawing on all the picturesque potentialities of such a strange, un-social type. This is one possible line of development from such a conception as the Pancake Woman; the other is that towards the Peasants' Feast in Zurich, where no single extravagant figure claims all the beholder's attention.

The elements in these two paintings in Philadelphia are not yet held together by the enveloping tone, as in the Peasants' Feast. Yet they are markedly subdued in colour, when compared, say, with Frans Hals' Merry Company in New York. One must not imagine the latter as too colourful; but it is paler, lighter in tone than these works of Brouwer's and has more colour more evenly distributed. The Pancake Woman comes closest to Hals: it is as if Brouwer has taken such a painting as this Merry Company as his starting point, but has then gone his own way, in respect both to colour and to subject, choosing a slightly comical figure, distantly comparable to Hals' comedians. Soon, however, Brouwer will begin to prefer subjects taken altogether from everyday life.

The striking main colour of the Merry Company is the mauve of the woman's bodice, heavily embroidered in white and gold and dull green. This refined mauve determines the total impression of the painting, and mauve is also the most prominent colour in these compositions by Brouwer. The baking woman wears a raspberry-coloured jacket (a beautifully refined and toneful colour) and a lilac-white skirt; her counterpart wears a dull green blouse, and has a cherry-red hat on his queer head. (The farmer in the Peasants' Feast wears a similar hat; this colour accent, favoured by Brouwer and used by him with emphasis in even later paintings, is a residue of the local-colour fashion.) These are the most striking colours in this palely tinted work. If one compares the light background of the left half of this painting with the uniformly sustained tone of the Peasants' Feast, it appears that the Pancake Man stands between the other two; the partition of planks is farther to the front than the light wall in the Pancake Woman, and the dark depth of the place is continued above the partition.

The drawing is much better in the Pancake Man, and the details are more finished: not only the curious face of the man, but also his odd leggings, and the pots and pans in the foreground in which the great still-life painter already shows his hand. The foreground exhibits a more marked variation of technique in contrast to the broader, more sketchy treatment of the group in the background. Some of the requisites of the Peasants' Feast are already evident. There is, for example, a large hat, here hanging on the chair behind the man's back, and badly worn, as the rest of his clothing (unlike the elegant head-dress of the fashionable guest in the Peasants' Feast). Behind this same chair is a greedy child who is up to his ears in pancake. What pleasure

74

39. PANCAKE MAN
Courtesy of the John G. Johnson Art Coll., Philadelphia

40. FIGHT OVER CARDS
Mauritshuis, The Hague

Brouwer must have taken in painting this greedy youngster! The four older people behind him, suggested in quick strokes rather than carefully delineated, are grossly involved in their pancakes and drink.

Brouwer's gradual evolution also appears in the colour. Again the man is wearing a purple-violet coat, which, set off against the red of the cap and the cuffs, appears somewhat warmer and stronger. (Is he wearing perhaps an old soldier's jacket—could he at one time have been a soldier?) There is some more colour in the still-life at his feet: the brown of the jug, and the red and orange of the pan; while the immense round jug of the man drinking in the background is brick-red. The rest is all in tune with these colours.

These two pictures in the Johnson Collection are the only works by Brouwer that can be regarded with certainty as predecessors of the Peasants' Feast. (They measure 28.38×43.37 and 33.75×27.81 cm., and in view of this discrepancy in format between height and width are surely not companion pieces.) They give on the one hand a clear picture of the master's pro-

41-43. FIGHT OVER CARDS (DETAILS, ACTUAL SIZE)
Mauritshuis, The Hague

gress toward this major work, and on the other hand a less clear picture of his deliberate departure from the example of Hals, his search for a form and content of his own. It is now doubly evident that, as has already been argued above, not one of the clumsy, dull paintings which have been regarded as early Brouwers can be so regarded any longer.

There is, however, one picture of an entirely different type which also appears to stem from this period of Brouwer's activity, few as are the points of contact with the works already discussed: the *Fight over Cards* (Bode 29) in the Mauritshuis (25.5×34 cm.). Since it is an outdoor scene, it makes different demands on the ability of the young artist. The light in this open space must remain even, there being no occasion for romantic lighting effects, no shadowy background, no dimming tonality. It has the uniform, bright tone of a summer's day with a lightly overcast sky; in contrast to those set indoors, this scene becomes brighter as it recedes. The landscape on the right with the grey-brown tower-ruin is painted in a greyish-green; but the whole foreground, as well as the mass on the left of the house and the bare, dead tree trunks are of an earthen-brown. The figures are kept to a fainter tone too, less colourful than the interior scenes, and suited to open-air light: the rough-neck in the centre with pale yellow breeches, light blue-green jacket and the mordant blue-green beret on his head, and the white head-dress of the peasant woman wearing a purplish garment afford touches of colour and a higher light. The remarkable discipline of the canvas, maintained in spite of the vigorous action taking place, is a sign of Brouwer's work; as is the fact that the action in itself is not really vigorous, but has the tension of action checked or impending, so that full emphasis falls on the intense, conflicting passions. A man—because of the small slits in the knees of his breeches—reminiscent of the sixteenth century—one imagines that a down-and-out mercenary was intended—, a veritable gallows-bird, has been playing cards in front of an inn at a table with long benches. He has jumped up in a fury, upsetting the beer jug and scattering the cards; he lays hold of the hilt of his short sword; but a frantic old woman holds his arm back entreatingly and an unshaven old man hurries to help her. Opposite him sits his advers-ary, an older peasant, who is no less furious; he holds his unsheathed sword in his tense fist, but an old crone has thrown herself across the table and pushes him with both hands back onto the bench. These are the principals in this 'image of the times'; about them others are fighting out a row of their own, or looking on in consternation, or, like the two boys at the right end of the table, discussing the event critically or with amusement. In the right fore-corner three dirty, prickly pigs and a piglet appear, not, certainly, by accident, but with a clear emblematic meaning.

In the middle ground of this small panel are further instances illustrating the coarseness of country life; a man leans vomiting over the long arm of a well-sweep; while next to him a man, seen from the back, relieves himself with great unconcern, although one of a group of five

78

people. Further on, in front of the ramshackle fence of a decrepit manor house with a round, ruined tower, there is a commotion near a covered wagon; what it is about is not clear, on account of the exceptionally broad-sketchy manner in which Brouwer has painted the scene, in grey-greens: it is as indistinct as it would have been to the eye of the observer at such a distance.

A scene like this is no uncommon motif in the painting of the time; but when we compare it with paintings which can be considered its models, such as those of the older Fleming, David Vinckboons, who lived in Amsterdam, the young Adriaen's mastery comes out quite clearly: in the construction and management of the scene; in the sober yet powerful intensity of the action. Similar scenes by Vinckboons, typically Flemish in origin and character—did not events like those depicted take place far more often in Flanders than in the long-pacified surroundings of Haarlem?—show many events, painted in an unquiet, uniformly strong colour scheme, but no single event dominates the picture. Vinckboons, like Brouwer, portrays the fierce passions on the faces of his figures, but in an exaggerated and conventional way. Particularly in his older work faces, porcelain-smooth, and round in the manner of the sixteenth century, alternate with caricatured toughs and drunkards. How differently this is treated by Brouwer. Each of his figures is a person in his own right and is cast for a particular, clearly defined and logical part in the play. According to the notions of the day the scene is a farce, but it brings forward the human elements, the inner conflict of each person so strongly, that we are more shocked than amused. What a frightful scoundrel Brouwer has drawn as his chief figure—how terrible the face—here is a man who would stop at nothing to satisfy his cruel lusts.

Vinckboons was not unknown in Haarlem. It is said that he interested Frans Hals in genre painting. This theory is not entirely satisfactory[1]; Hals could have found his incentive closer at hand in the work of the older Haarlem masters such as Cornelis Cornelisz. and van Mander. But with regard to Brouwer the connection is more convincing. Vinckboons' art was widely known through prints and had considerable influence. Esaias van de Velde, somewhat older than Brouwer, certainly profited from it. Vinckboons, like van de Velde himself, had been a pupil of Gillis van Coninxloo; the latter put a strong stamp on van de Velde's work, particularly his landscapes, a genre which Coninxloo had reduced to a special hackneyed stereotype. Curiously the influence of the Elsheimer landscape was at one time strongly felt in Vinckboons' and Esaias' work, while his other followers treated his style as a formula. With the construction of landscapes by the more independent Brouwer, who never took over anybody else's formula, the question of Elsheimer's influence does not arise. Brouwer's subjects, more than his landscape

[1] It is not to be denied, however, that the curious Outdoor Party in Berlin-Dahlem, almost universally ascribed to Hals as his earliest work, goes back to a print by C. J. Visser after a drawing by Vinckboons dated 1608. (See Korneel Goossens, 'David Vinckeboons', Antwerpen-'s-Gravenhage, 1954, p. 92).

settings, go back to Vinckboons' work, not his work in those years but that of ten to twenty years earlier, scenes of country life with figures on about the same scale as those in the Fight over Cards. These, by way of engraved copies, could have served to inspire Brouwer; but in this case too it is clear how far Brouwer has outstripped the example. His mastery appears in the exceptionally trenchant characterization of his subjects, the staging and dramatization of the picture, the refined choice of colour and tone, and the inventive, precise brushwork.

The four works which have been considered (the Pancake Woman, the Pancake Man, the Peasants' Feast, and the Fight over Cards) reflect, in this order, Brouwer's development not only into a master in complete control of his technical means for expressing what he wished, just as he wished to express it; but a development also toward mental maturity and self-control, which enable him, through subordination and elimination, to achieve conciseness, unity and comprehension. The amusing scene in the Peasants' Feast of the man flirting with the farmer's wife, and the greedy child are so treated as not to detract from the principal motif: the meal itself with its picturesque chief figures of farmer and fiddler. By a slightly stronger lighting the rough man in the centre foreground of the Fight over Cards is made, in all his bestiality, into the express subject of this painting.

These are the only works which can with conviction be ascribed to this period. They illustrate Brouwer's development step by step, and for this reason they have been extensively treated here. They exhibit not only the artist's inner growth, but also a number of distinctive qualities which will be of importance in his later development: his true character is already present in outline. These qualities, moreover, are the touchstone for the correctness of our delimitation of Brouwer's work.

It must now have become more than evident that these unquestionable attributions leave no place in Brouwer's œuvre for the clumsy, so-called youthful works ascribed to him even by Bode and Böhmer. There is no longer any reason to attribute to Brouwer these paintings, not in themselves without merit: for instance the landscapes with quite a number of small figures evenly distributed among different scenes, anecdotal and sometimes a little ironic, but not dramatized. There is no connection between Brouwer's Fight over Cards and the Peasants' Kermis 14 with the man lying out full length on a bench (Böhmer 7), or the Peasants' Kermis with the 15 pair of lovers under a tree and on the left a soldier seen from the back (ibid. 8), or the Ninepin Players at the Farm (ibid. 10). Nor, if these works are repetitions—and different copies of 7 and 10 are in existence—is there any connection between the originals and genuine work by Brouwer.

These four paintings by Brouwer show that from the beginning he bore the distinctive marks of his artistry in him: an intuitive grasp of composition, colour and characterization, a self-control that achieves strong accents and effects within the limits of the normal. He characterizes rather than caricatures, even if, in the case of the angry farmer in the Pancake Woman, he slips into youthful exaggeration—if, indeed, this detail does not indicate that this painting is not the original.

Once this point in Brouwer's career has been reached, many possibilities open up.

2. LATER YEARS IN HOLLAND

It stands to reason that in those first years in Holland Brouwer painted more than the four works discussed above. The exceptional craftsmanship and versatility of these paintings, as well as their scrupulous finish, bespeak a life not of debauchery but of concentrated dedication to his work. Yet no other works are known which could have originated in this period. Only one work seems to come close to the Peasants' Feast, although presumably of a later rather than an earlier date: the powerful scene of the *Tooth Puller*; portraying a man who is extracting a tooth in front of a village house.[1] This picture, like the Pancake Man, is dominated by a single large figure, similarly seen from the side. The very solid composition is marked by strong lines, or rather channels of direction. If not quite so pronounced, this element is also present in the earlier works. Probably Brouwer did not construct his compositions systematically according to such a plan; rather, following an infallible sense of balance and rhythm, a sense of the value and necessity of a taut structure, he created a foundation by means of which the picture acquired space, grandeur and clarity. It is delightful to take cognizance of the system of horizontals and verticals, of parallels and anti-parallels, and of the exactly contrasting small divergences which provide the scaffolding for the scene. Observe the anti-parallel lines of the plank in the right foreground and the pole through the basket on the left; the horizontals of the plank on the barrel and the strongly lit tent-roof farther back; the striking bright square surface of the placard: everywhere there are elements controlling the direction. We are confronted with a composition built up by means of components in tension, independent of the representation.

This characteristic is also to be observed in the Peasants' Feast, but less clearly developed. We would, therefore, suppose the Tooth Puller to have been painted a little later. It also shows development towards portraying a clearly specified moment; a tendency in this direction had already appeared in the threat of action by the fierce central figure in the Fight over Cards; but now the tooth is indeed being drawn. The surgeon is doing his job in a business-like way, with the complete concentration called for by a difficult task. The patient submits to treatment, his whole body tense, supporting himself with his fist against the top of the barrel. The surgeon's

[1] Formerly in the Komter Collection (Bode 26); in 1932 it was in the hands of the art dealer Abels in Cologne. Known to me only through reproductions.

81

grinning wife stands behind: her face, the upper part concealed by a black hood, manifests devilish pleasure in the patient's suffering; a few frowsy strands of hair are showing, and a bit of white seen through a slit in her dress just under her chin almost suggests a goat's beard. Behind the barrel two children look on, their faces devoid of intelligence. The one on the left, smirking, whispers something to the girl on the right, who is thoroughly enjoying the sight of the peasant's tortures. Behind this satanic scene the peasant village appears in a warm summer light, giving onto a landscape view reminiscent of the Fight over Cards in the Mauritshuis, but simpler and nearer and accordingly of a grander vision.

13   When we compare this felicitous composition with the *Quacksalver* at Karlsruhe (Bode 24), it is difficult to credit the notion that the latter derives from a Brouwer original of this same period. If this should yet prove to be the case, the distance between original and imitation must have been very great. The same is true of other related compositions, constructed on a diagonal, with a group of people on the one side,—some with queer, misshapen bodies—and a view on the other. Brouwer's sensibility lay outside the scope of his followers; in their hands his keen characterization deteriorated into gross caricature.

The *Peasants Dancing*, formerly in the Schloss Collection (Bode 23), makes a somewhat better impression. In the way the scene is built up, it reminds us of the Tooth Puller. But it has no chief figure, and really no point. And the rendering is too coarse to be worthy of Brouwer. We shall return to this painting later.

A change now takes place in Brouwer's style. He turns away from too great premeditation in handling his motifs as well as in his manner of expression, in his characterization as well as in his brush-writing, and in the relationship of colour to tone. The structural elements in his compositions are not so emphatic as in the Tooth Puller, but continue to control, no less essentially, the appearance of his work. His preference now runs to interiors with numerous, relatively large figures, freely arranged in space. There is no longer any one exceptional or dominating figure, nor does an action furnish the central motif. Men play, drink, smoke—and suffer the consequences. Every man is endowed with individuality, not as a freak, but by means of the acuteness with which his personality is built up and expressed. Precisely this distinguished Brouwer from his older Haarlem contemporaries such as Dirck Hals or Pot, or younger ones such as Jan Miense Molenaar, Judith Leyster or Adriaen van Ostade. Brouwer individualizes his genre-figures as strongly as Frans Hals does the subjects of his portraits. In this process he is continually changing his means and manner of expression—as Rembrandt also did: for these two great artists such problems were not merely technical ones, but belonged to the realms of direct aesthetic creativity and of artistic pleasure.

In this way we can assemble the group of six paintings next discussed: a *Tavern Interior* in the

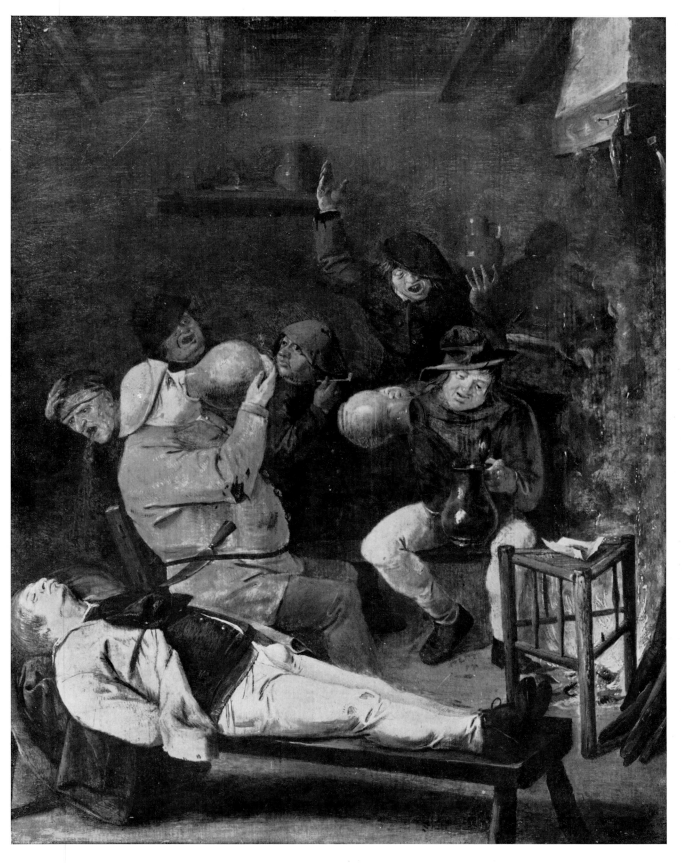

44. TAVERN INTERIOR
Museum Boymans-van Beuningen, Rotterdam

83

Museum Boymans-van Beuningen in Rotterdam, the Slaughter Feast in Schwerin, the Smokers in Kassel, the Feast of the Cook, of which one example is at present in the Boston Museum of Fine Arts, Peasants Guzzling in the Mauritshuis in The Hague, and The Moerdijk Peasants in the Markus Collection, Scarsdale, New York. In these pictures not one figure is particularly conspicuous; each, although a member of the group, retains his independence; none has a special function: the artist no longer need rely on such means to achieve subordination. No one is caricatured, except by virtue of the situation to which his drinking or smoking has brought him. Such situations seem especially to attract the painter, probably because of the freedom with which men then express themselves.

It is difficult to insist on a sequence for these pictures. The Rotterdam panel might be the
44 oldest (Bode 21; 34.8 × 26 cm.). The sharpness of the drawing, and also the fire on the right recall the Pancake Man in Philadelphia, and there is some connection with the Peasants' Feast. But the colour here is livelier, the tone is lighter and the people are less bizarre, at least as types. The colour scheme is again one of great refinement. Across the foreground lies the lightly coloured area of the drunkard: he is in yellowish-white breeches and a pale violet jacket, under which he wears a green-blue waistcoat; on it is his blue beret. There he lies, sleeping his drunk off, his head on a grey-blue jacket. Just behind him is the dull orange-red jacket of the fat drinker, who is raising a great beer jug to his wide open mouth with both hands. The man on the right wears a green jacket. He pours beer from an earthenware jug into a pewter one, with a curiously mollified expression. There is little colour in the rest of the picture. In addition there are four strange characters, each a wonderful type in itself. Like the similar figure in the Peasants' Feast, the man standing in the right rear has his arms raised; and on his right is a small, round smoker wearing a queer hat with holes in it. In this picture smoking appears as a more innocent pastime than it will in later pictures: here it is a novelty, something unusual, which receives all one's attention. The tobacco came in squares of paper, such as the one on the three-legged stool by the fire.

This painting represents a more mature and above all a freer stage than the previous one. The composition is freer not only in that Brouwer has grouped his figures farther toward the back, but also because of the style of painting, which allows great contrasts between fine, precise finish and sketchy notation. This occurs even in different parts having similar value: the sketched-in head, for example, of the man with the jug to his mouth over against the more finished faces around him. The rear wall and ceiling are represented in what is for Brouwer an unusually thin, sketchy way.

45 Many of these distinctive features are to be observed in the *Slaughter Feast* in Schwerin (Bode 13; 34 × 37 cm.), but with the space more clearly represented, and a more detailed background. Smoking plays no role here; the subject is a slaughter feast (the pig's head is on the table) that

45. SLAUGHTER FEAST
Staatliches Museum, Schwerin

has been enjoyed in abundance; at least two of the banqueters can no longer keep it up; but the fat peasant woman on the left promises to be equal to her enormous glass of beer. Again there is a light-coloured figure in the foreground, this time asleep across a barrel-top. His body is a marked line in the composition; and this line is turned back into the picture by a white cat, eating in the centre foreground. This manner of handling a salient line which runs toward the edge of the picture and, if unchecked, would lead the eye outside it is characteristic of Brouwer.

This is the largest panel of the group. Perhaps this fact led to a somewhat broader manner of painting. Did Brouwer then, for the sake of a change or for practice, decide to try an entirely

II different style, such as that of the *Smokers* in Kassel (Bode 18; 25 × 37 cm.), which is executed with an almost academic carefulness, in plastically distinct curves and arches? The background apparently did not interest him, since he left it an even grey, except for the indispensable view on the right out over the lower half of the door, across which a man is as usual leaning. Near him are a child in a barrel chair and a little old man and woman—what brings them there, one wonders? The props of chairs, crockery, and such are limited, compared to the earlier paintings; the full emphasis falls on the seven men who are sitting together, three of them given over to the enjoyment of smoking.

Again we are struck by the clarity, tranquillity and large scale of the composition; even more remarkable is the plasticity of every part of each body—note, for example, the carefully modelled knee at the left—and especially of the heads. (The peculiar optical consequence is that one imagines the painting to be larger than it actually is, much larger, say, than the Rotterdam Tavern Interior, which is in fact only slightly smaller.) The people here are eminently normal, nor are they down-at-heel vagrants. It looks rather like a portrait of a group of men who differ considerably from one another. One, with his head on his hand, has fallen asleep. What sureness suddenly appears in the painting, and also in the painting of the objects, the stick of burning wood, the jugs, the pot! Everything about this plastic, almost academic representation is too emphatic not to be deliberate. But why? Perhaps it was the result of a wager or a competition with an older painter, such as Moeyaert. Who knows? The colours, in rich variety, are somewhat stronger and are more wide-spread; this too is a consequence of the altered conception of the painting, which tends to bring everything fully and more equally into its own. The general tone remains a red-purple; the figure in the right foreground is in green and blue: grey-green waist-coat, blue sleeve and green breeches, with a yellow cap. The corresponding figure on the left is wearing a brown coat and a purple-red cap, a bit of pink breeches is showing above his pink knee, and again there is a blue-green stocking. The middle figure, who is filling his pipe as he talks quietly, shows a pink sleeve protruding from a brown jacket.

Thus all combines to lend this picture an almost sedate air; the characters are relaxing peacefully, without excess.

This painting does not stand entirely apart. Brouwer applies the same technique more playfully and subtly, with more liberty and variety, in the far more complicated compositio   the
33 Feast of the Cook, of which at least three examples are known, one of which is in Boston.[1] Here too the participants are feasting genially. Again there is the strong accent of a large, lightly coloured figure in the foreground, but now seen from behind: the cook, with his white jacket and yellow cap and the cloth hanging over the bottom of his chair. Magnificent is the wide curve of the right arm lifted high, continuing in the yellow earthen Raeren-jug. The cook is wearing

(¹) See above, chapter: Repetitions, copies, imitations, p. 57.

II. Smokers
Staatliche Kunstsammlungen, Kassel

green breeches; so is the man with the orange-red cap in the barrel chair. All round is a grey tonality, in which the pewter of the big jug in the left foreground stands out.

The scheme of the composition has become more subtle: because he is seen from behind, the fanciful foreground figure who attracts the beholder's attention by his light colours, also serves as an effective means of drawing the eye inward into the scene. The post on the right, moreover, has the function of creating depth. The grinning face directly under the cook's raised right arm recalls the face in the middle of the Kassel *Smokers*, having the same function in the composition; while the man's features would appear to be the same as the cook's. This too points to a connection between these paintings.

Next comes the *Peasants Guzzling* in the Mauritshuis (Bode 14; 19.5 × 26.5 cm.). The com- III position is almost simple: a group round a table. But this would have led to one or more figures shown with their backs toward the beholder; instead Brouwer has placed the figure of the 46 drunken mother in the foreground, she is leaning forward, nauseated; her child grabs her arm 47 anxiously: apparently the child is the only one shocked by his mother's behaviour. Again we 48 see a fellow standing with raised arms behind the group, holding a full glass in one hand; and 49 we have again the customary scene near the open door, this time with five people, thinly and somewhat vaguely painted. Everyone has had his fill. The wonderful fat peasant on the right has collapsed, stupified, onto his three-cornered chair. Opposite him, in a barrel chair, sits another drinker, cheerfully grinning, with one pipe in his hand and another stuck in his cap. The chalk marks on the back of his chair show the score that must be settled. A young fellow squints out from under his soft hat, sucking in contentment on his pipe, which lies in the pipkin on the table. The older woman next to him, with her frightfully pale face, appears to be singing, either by herself or with her genial neighbour, who is raising a jug to his mouth. The term 'genial', however, does not fit this scene very well, although at first glance the besotted company might seem farcical. Brouwer was no joker—at least as an artist. Perhaps in the first instance such a scene was intended to be amusing; but in the course of painting it Brouwer was diverted by his sarcastic, harsh—or was it really his compassionate—spirit into a vein of relentless candour: far from finding amusement in this bestiality, he chastises by concealing nothing of its depravity. The group formed by the woman on the floor, her collapsed husband and their helpless child is the chief motif of this scene and of its composition. It draws a diagonal line, leaving a space open in the foreground to receive the woman when she rolls over, and perhaps her husband as well. The composition is not so simple as at first appeared.

Each of these faces deserves to be studied in turn. With what infinite variety the master portrays the drunk: each man is drawn not only in his own form of intoxication, but with a personality entirely his own.

This is also a small masterpiece as regards colour and technique. The manner is exception-

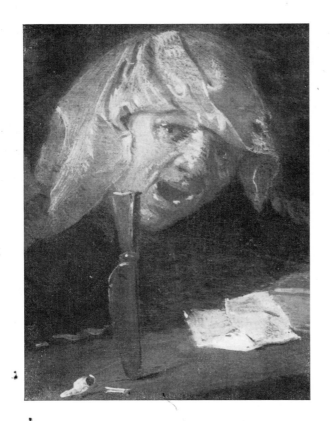

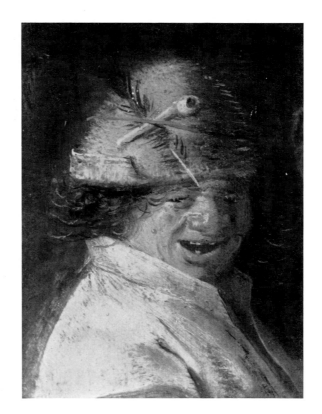

46-48. Peasants Guzzling (details)
Mauritshuis, The Hague

88

III. Peasants Guzzling

Mauritshuis, The Hague

49. PEASANTS GUZZLING (DETAIL)
Mauritshuis, The Hague

ally fine and sensitive; the surface is partly covered with even touches of quiet colours, again dominated by a purplish tone. The strongest light is concentrated in the beautifully painted head-kerchief of the woman on the floor. The colours in the group of husband and wife have been exquisitely assembled: a dull yet deep wax-red skirt with a green lining, against the child's grey jacket, and a slightly darker green bodice; the man wears grey breeches and a pale-violet coat above a deep-blue vest. His hat is a cherry red, and the sleeve of the boy smoking, behind the woman's white head-dress, is dull blue. Together with the brown jug on the floor at the right, these are the most salient colours in a composition which for the rest is kept to a tranquil tone.

The so-called *Moerdijk Peasants* (now in the Markus Collection in Scarsdale, New York; Bode 17; 30 × 25.5 cm.) also belongs to this group. It is, like the Kassel painting, surprisingly IV smaller than one would expect from the reproduction, because of the closed, monumental rendering of form. We are confronted with a new experiment in composition: the group consists of two rows of three people each, placed diagonally across the composition, facing each other; at the same time a triangle is formed by the two foremost men and the standing

89

figure behind them. The strongest light is now concentrated in a much smaller area—the leg in the left foreground—and is taken up again by the delightful white cat asleep on the right. The tone is subdued and rather cool. The man on the left in the yellow-white breeches wears a blue jacket; the figure opposite him is held to steel-blue; while the mauve and purple so typical of Brouwer appear in the standing man, who is lighting his pipe in the pipkin held out by the man seated across from him. What a simple, natural way to solve the problem of the apex of the triangle.

In this picture smoking has become a special activity carried on with concentration by a group apparently assembled for the purpose,—as has not been the case before. There may be a connection between this fact and the name of the painting, The Moerdijk Peasants, which appears under an old printed reproduction by P. Malenvie.[1]

Smoking, in Brouwer's first works, is as harmless a pleasure as it is today, but, in the later ones, has become a narcotic ceremony, in which the smoker, isolated while in the midst of his fellow-addicts, is entirely given over to hallucinations.[2] This change is not, of course, a development of technique, but reflects the further experience of the painter. The name of this painting could point to the fact that Brouwer painted such a scene in the course of his journey from Haarlem to Antwerp, near the Moerdijk[3], that is to say south of the great rivers. Here he may have gained his first knowledge of tobacco with hemp added, the 'belladonna' as referred to by Timmermans, smoked to produce hallucinations and visions. If this is the case, the painting becomes a document of the transition from the Dutch to the Flemish period. It seems to be the latest of the paintings described so far, and demonstrates the increasing ability of the young master to raise each figure to the level of an independent personality without letting the composition fall apart. Even the small white cat in the lower right corner is, as the beginning of a diagonal which runs to the head of the standing smoker, a point of force, and an essential element which cannot be spared.

Although there are reasons to consider the Tavern Interior in the Museum Boymans-van Beuningen as the earliest painting in this group, and The Moerdijk Peasants as the last, to be dated after Brouwer's departure from Haarlem, yet there are no conclusive arguments in favour of any particular sequence among the six. A young artist is experimenting again and again, just as Rembrandt is doing in these years. He does not wish to commit himself finally to a single definitive form.

([1]) Following Schmidt-Degener, p. 10. This critic sees the painting as a transitional piece done by Brouwer on his journey from Antwerp to the north; but this opinion depends on the unwarranted assumption of a first Antwerp period before the painter came north.

([2]) See above, p. 26.

([3]) The Moerdijk is a small village on the Dutch side of the Hollands Diep, the broad expanse of water separating the province of 'Holland' from Brabant. A ferry was the most important means of communication between the north and south banks, so would serve Brouwer on his way to Antwerp. There is a bridge now.

IV. The Moerdijk Peasants

F. Markus Collection, Scarsdale (N.Y.)

3. FIRST YEARS IN ANTWERP

Should the *Card Players* in Antwerp (Bode 19; 25 × 39 cm.) be included in the group just 50 discussed? The composition is different. There are comparatively fewer figures, and these 51 have been moved to the left: in the emptier space each object receives an emphasis of its own. 52 Apparently Brouwer now was experimenting in all directions. Later this scheme of composition with the chief group moved to one side would become a favourite of Brouwer's; but he may well have tried it earlier. The emphasis on separate forms harks back to the Dutch period. The thin card player seen from the back emphatically closes the left half off from the rest of the picture; he at the same time is inseparably connected to it by the diagonal line which runs from his back over the cask to the stick of wood on the lower right. The little white dog recalls the white cat which occupies the same place in The Moerdijk Peasants, and it has the same function in the composition as has the cat in the Slaughter Feast in Schwerin, but in a more complicated fashion: the line of the dog's back runs parallel to the diagonal from upper right to lower left, and—surely no accident—with the light left thigh of the card player in the centre of the picture. The other diagonal, running from this man's back over the cask to the stick of wood leaning against it, turns upwards again along the dog's back.

The main group offers a pleasant enough scene: a quiet game of cards between two lean men absorbed in their play. Similarly pleasant are the smiling innkeeper behind them, filling his pipe, and the older woman looking over the latter's shoulder. The typing of this foursome is clever. The player on the right is showing his four aces, enjoying everyone's surprise; his opponent is taking in his presumed loss, his cards still hidden in his left hand, while he raises the jug to his mouth with his right. The expression of the onlookers suggests that he is holding back a surprise.

In the upper right hand corner, however, between the door and the fireplace there is an entirely different group; at least one guest lying on a bench is overcome with drink. It seems that there must always be something of that sort in Brouwer!

The principal figure is, although dimmed, still the strongest light in the picture; he is painted in shades of violet and blue. The colour pattern is again subtle. The basket with provisions, including a dead duck, in the lower left corner, is beautifully painted: the artist again shows himself here to be a master of still-life.

The exceptional leanness of the main figures is of course no coincidence. So far Brouwer's people have been rather too portly than too slim. Here this device has a powerfully spacious effect on the composition, as was probably the painter's intention. These lanky figures take up less room, so that the effect of space is enhanced by this relative openness. The relationship to space is an important problem for Brouwer; he seeks more and more to immerse his pictures in space. Thus we may view The Moerdijk Peasants and this painting as two representative facets of Brouwer's art at the time of his removal from Holland to Flanders.

Remotely connected with The Moerdijk Peasants is the somewhat wooden composition *La Chanson à Boire* in the Petit Palais in Paris (Bode 50; 30 × 21 cm.). Perhaps it is a copy: the beautiful qualities of the colour and tone notwithstanding, the clumsy drawing, as in the hanging arm of the man on the right, rules it out as an original (See p. 111).

But it is of better quality than the *Three Men* (Bode 43) which came into the hands of the art dealer Katz in Dieren from the collection of M. van Gelder in Ukkel, Belgium. Two of the three men are sitting with stout jugs by a table and tabouret. The third stands behind them, head bent beneath a black cap. Elements of Brouwer, yes; an original, no. The burliness of the figure in front puts one in mind of the singers in La Chanson à Boire.

The *Drinking Song*. The small panel with a peasant pawing a woman, in the Bredius Museum in The Hague (27 × 34.5 cm.), does not have the qualities of an original to a convincing degree, although Dr. Bredius was of the opinion that it was mentioned in seventeenth century documents.[1] The composition is certainly Brouwer's. In the left foreground is a thick-set loutish peasant vigorously exploring beneath the skirts of a woman no less chubby than he. They are unaware of the four men on the right and a fifth behind a partition, chuckling over the spectacle. In later years this motif recurs in more explicit, spectacular form in the painting in the collection of Sir Edmund Bacon in the National Gallery, London.[2]

If Brouwer declared on March the fourth, 1632, that he had himself painted a Peasants Dancing which had already been in Rubens' possession for a year, and that he had painted this scene only once, it follows that the painting must have been done either at the beginning of his Antwerp period or even earlier. This painting is not known, but the composition may have come down to us in a drawing of 1659 by Matthijs van den Bergh, which certainly represents a painting by Brouwer.[3]

(1) Herein Dr. Bredius found mention made of a painting by Brouwer, in which a peasant was shown putting his hand under a woman's skirt. But this subject occurs more than once, and the description would not aid in distinguishing between a copy and an original. Dr. Hofstede de Groot reproduced this archival discovery by Bredius in his Kritisches Verzeichnis (No. 68) as 'proof'.

(2) Another panel in the National Gallery (29 × 22 cm.), which (justly) is not highly thought of there, shows three lads carousing, drinking and sleeping in a cellar room. In the bulkiness and lumpiness of the figures it seems to be related to the painting in the Bredius Museum. This type of space does not appear, it is true, in any other painting by Brouwer; but the sleeping youth on the right could be a predecessor of the boy sleeping off his drunk in the picture in the Wallace Collection, were it not that the latter is a more presentable youth and is also better painted. One thing and another suggests the nice, correctly finished work of a later painter, who worked with Brouwer's motifs, rather than a copy of a work by Brouwer himself (See p. 111).

(3) Bode accepted this as almost certain, since van den Bergh, as a son of Rubens' bailiff, grew up in Rubens' house. But this does not really prove much: as early as 1646 van den Bergh was in the guild at Alkmaar, where he was also living in 1659. He did not draw this scene from memory, but might have been following a drawing he had made earlier.

50. CARD PLAYERS
Koninklijk Museum voor Schone Kunsten, Antwerp

51-52. CARD PLAYERS (DETAILS, ACTUAL SIZE)

53. MATTHIJS VAN DEN BERGH, PEASANTS DANCING, AFTER BROUWER
Staatliche Museen, Berlin-Dahlem

A few of the figures in this drawing appear also in the Peasants Dancing formerly in the Schloss Collection (Bode 23; already discussed above, page 82; a number of other versions are known). Compared to the Fight over Cards in the Mauritshuis, this important composition is more closely packed with more numerous, somewhat larger figures; the farmers' houses on the left are more heavily painted, and the village perspective on the right is less vague. The connection with similar compositions originating in the school of Bruegel is clear—but equally clear is Brouwer's very personal style. In the foreground lies a man on his knees, vomiting. A rather slow dance is taking place around a child sitting on the ground: five people are dancing with bent knees and mostly with bent backs. There are a good many bystanders. In a somewhat 53 later composition, the one drawn by van den Bergh, Brouwer reworked a few of these elements. Thus he took over the principal dancer and his closest neighbours, using them in a more elaborate row-dance, which he placed further to the right and much deeper in the middle distance. This goes hand in hand with the striving, already observed, for greater spaciousness, for immersing the representation in the surrounding space. It also creates an open, somewhat empty foreground: in the left a funny old couple sits embracing; another old couple further to the rear centre is dancing; and a disgusting event is introduced in the right foreground, where a man lies vomiting over a bench, while a pig slobbers up the vomit and a toddler sits looking on.

If this reproduces the composition of the painting which Rubens got from Brouwer and apparently valued highly, he still does not appear to have let it inspire him in his treatment

94

of the same theme. Brouwer depicts peasant dances strictly according to life, in all their heavy ungainliness and clumsy turgidness. Not so Rubens, whose peasant men and women, only sometimes dressed in their own costumes, are Arcadians, like Hooft's country people; he is concerned with the representation of an undulating rhythm which carries everything along in its wild impetus, checked only by its circular course. Brouwer's concern was with the relentless reproduction of reality, and preferably of reality in its more raw, uncouth aspects; he was preoccupied with truth. In this respect these two masters were poles apart; and it explains why the younger had little desire to become involved in the courtly surroundings of the prince of painters and his essentially aesthetic approach toward his subjects.

4. LATER YEARS IN ANTWERP

Works of a very divergent nature thus present themselves as creations from the beginning of Brouwer's stay in Antwerp. One must expect this from the experimentally inclined Adriaen Brouwer, and it indicates the difficulty of arranging the work of the last six years of his life. In dealing with a master whose nature was lively, diligent, receptive and intensely conscientious, there will be no question of coming to a standstill in development, or of a gradual, systematic development towards a goal which, although unforeseen, was present as a tendency from the very beginning, as in Rembrandt's case. Works from 1637 will certainly differ from those of about 1632—but the course followed will not be a straight, direct one. The artist will try increasingly to envelop the representation in a surrounding atmosphere, to shroud it in tone, with steadily less glaring light or colour accents; so that what emerges is a true, tranquil and beautiful unity with finesse in colour and tone, with precise still life painting alternating with larger areas painted in a broader style, with sharply varied and individualized portrayals of man; while beauty's seductive cloak will be used to conceal a portrait of human indignity. The trend will be from the contained, closed, precisely painted representation of form to a more economical, freer, broader, more fluently suggestive style, bringing the personal handwriting of the master more and more to the fore, while the purely technical problems of accounting for forms recede in importance.

There is no external evidence for dating the later works; except for the fact that de Heem's presence in The Smokers in the Metropolitan Museum places that work in 1636 or 1637.[1] This

(¹) Jan Davidz. de Heem, of Utrecht, became a member of the Antwerp St. Luke's Guild in 1636, and in 1637 was a citizen of Antwerp. This establishes the fact that The Smokers could not have been painted earlier than 1636, not much more than a year, therefore, before the end of Brouwer's activity. De Heem, born in 1606, was a contemporary of Brouwer; when he came to Antwerp he was already a mature master of elegant and excellent still-lifes of flowers and fruits; he apparently expected to find in Antwerp a richer abundance of his 'material'.

54. THE SMOKERS (DETAIL)
The Metropolitan Museum of Art, New York (The Michael Friedsam Coll., 1931)

work confirms the expectations just described. It serves the same function for the Antwerp period that the Peasants' Feast in the Ruzicka Foundation does for the Dutch period; a comparison of the two shows what an enormous distance the master had covered in these eight or nine years.

V The importance of *The Smokers* (Bode 117; 46 × 36.5 cm.) for the study of Brouwer's life was given in the first chapter (p. 23), with an extensive description of the scene. What follows is a discussion from the point of view of painting. This picture is decidedly not colourful; hung

54 among its Flemish contemporaries in the New York museum, it looks colourless and dark. (Cleaning and restoration might change this somewhat, but not significantly.) This tonality is the artist's conscious choice in all his later work, a respect in which he is more like his Dutch than his Flemish contemporaries.

The breeches of the chief figure, Brouwer himself, are violet with red buttons, a red bow under the knee and red laces: the jacket is a warm brown with red lapels. De Heem wears the

V. THE SMOKERS

The Metropolitan Museum of Art, New York (Michael Friedsam Collection, 1931)

sober black of a burgher, with wide white collar and cuffs. The scoundrel next to him wears a dark yellow hat; the unsavoury character on the left behind Brouwer's chair is in dull blue with a grey felt hat. The red-brown jug in the foreground is a restrained colour accent—and that is all the colour there is. Delightful is the freedom of the painter's touch, which, under this distinguished craftsman's control, changes according to the material to be represented, the form, or the place in the composition. An example of this is the still-life of tub, broom and jug in the lower left corner; and the contrasting white cloth that Brouwer is sitting on. The painter's touch becomes surprisingly broad, almost striped, in the treatment of Brouwer's breeches and jacket; but it is most surprising in the faces. Brouwer wished to paint a good likeness of de Heem, yet animated and integrated into the small comedy. Perhaps the painting was intended for him. Brouwer has captured the distance, unintentional on de Heem's part, between the newly arrived comrade from Utrecht and the rest of the company. Of his own head Brouwer has made a fantastic character study; unfortunately the left cheek is rather badly drawn. He did not stick at showing himself under the gratifying but baneful influence of the vile tobacco mixture (which he surely must have tried himself). Nor is the third friend, the middle figure, entirely free from this influence, but Brouwer has half hidden his face under the rising smoke, not, however, so that he is unrecognizable. The faces of the two rogues have been beautifully done. Oddly enough the one next to de Heem has been identified as Ostade, as recently as in the catalogue of the Flemish exhibition at the Royal Academy in London in 1927.[1]

These five men form a closed group, which fills the composition—and the space, as well. This is not in agreement with the previously noted tendency toward greater openness and spaciousness. But Brouwer painted as he thought the circumstances required, and did not feel bound

[1] The catalogue was following a statement in the catalogue of the Steengracht auction held in Paris on June the ninth, 1913. Here the traditional identification was given—with considerable reservation—by Frits Lugt, who prepared the catalogue. When he says: 'A droite, un personnage que l'on croit être Frans Hals; au fond, un fumeur, que la tradition indique comme Adriaen van Ostade; près de lui, un homme qui passe pour être le peintre Arie de Vois;' it is clear that he did not himself believe this identification, but he had to give it in the interest of the sale. On this occasion the painting brought no less than 426 500 gold franks which indicates how highly it was then valued. (Rembrandt's Bathsheba brought in 1 000 000 franks at the same sale.) In this catalogue Lugt cites the important passage about this painting from an article by W. Bürger (Thoré) in L'Artiste, nouvelle série, vol. VI, p. 58 (23 Jan. 1859). 'Le tableau est incomparablement le chef d'œuvre de Brouwer, et une des peintures les plus surprenantes de l'école hollandaise, un chef d'œuvre qu'on peut mettre à côté du Rembrandt le plus fougueux, le plus étrange, le plus solide, le plus magistral. Ce Brouwer ne craint pas même Rembrandt, comme puissance et originalité, comme énergie expressive, comme emportement d'exécution!' Further: 'car cette peinture, il faut la voir, comme, dans une autre sphère, il faut voir la Joconde de Léonard...'; and finally: 'Il se pourrait que les deux figures principales fussent des portraits, et que le tableau fût un souvenir de quelque partie de cabaret.' We may note in passing the remarkable opinion of Schmidt-Degener, who accepted the notion that the figure on the right was a portrait of Frans Hals; this is out of the question, since Frans Hals would have been about fifty-six years old in 1636. At the Oukerke auction at Haarlem in 1818 this painting brought 62 guilders, and in 1833 it was bought by Baron Steengracht from the collector J. de Vos for 490 guilders.

by theoretic niceties: here his subject led to a grouping together, to a closed and therefore to a monumental group. And this grouping became in itself a fascinating problem for the artist, one which he had apparently not encountered in his earlier work. This time the background of the comedy is not occupied by the scene of the drunkard leaning over the under-door, but by a couple who in a tender embrace walk away into the Kempen dune-landscape. In this picture Brouwer himself plays the leading part, as Jan Steen did so often in his pictures. Of all Brouwer's pictures this one comes nearest to Steen—but at the same time completely outstrips the Dutch Molière in his penetrating study of character.

Thus this painting is the echo of a pleasant episode out of the last years of Brouwer's life. But a man who paints with such enjoyment of his craft, and affection for it, a man who is able to put such a complicated representation on canvas with this artistry and sureness is hardly a run-down rake, a profligate or a libertine.

55   The *Back Operation* in Frankfort (Bode 113; 34 × 27 cm.) is closely related to this painting. It is similar in the closed group-composition, constricted space and scarceness of details. The figures are on approximately the same scale, if not a little larger. Brouwer could have used himself—with great latitude—as the model for the patient. The painting is in general less finely finished, except for a few places which particularly took Brouwer's imagination, such as the small still life on the shelf in the upper right-hand corner, and particularly the beautifully painted nude back, unique in Brouwer's œuvre, and, of course, the heads. The connoisseur of human reactions was certainly at work here. What a trio the patient, the surgeon and the woman attending, make! The patient has one eye closed, in a face distorted with pain, or perhaps rather with the fear of pain; the surgeon is engrossed in his responsible, careful work; and the woman is smiling nervously, all her attention focused on the operation. An empty jug hangs from her left hand, probably intended, once it has been filled, to console the patient with after the operation. A single detail like this fixes the entire episode: the woman is on her way to fetch a potion for the patient's after-care or consolation; she pauses to watch the course of the operation. Such a thing lends the representation liveliness and atmosphere.

This painting is lighter in tone than the one in New York because of the main motif, the naked back and the white shirt. Round about it is a quiet play of greys, greenish violets and browns. The surgeon wears a mat-blue hat.

56   The *Foot Operation*, also in Frankfort (Bode 112; 35 × 26 cm.) is related to the preceding
57   picture, but is still quite different. The group, less compact, has similarly been pushed into the
58   centre. The soldier-like patient has kept his hat on during his visit to the doctor. Again the latter is entirely taken up by his difficult work. The woman, here clearly his wife, grins diabolically at the patient, who does not move a muscle, thereby doing the old crone out of her sensational enjoyment. The manner of painting is bolder, yet more careful and more varied

98

55. BACK OPERATION
Staedelsches Kunstinstitut, Frankfort a.M.

99

56. FOOT OPERATION
Staedelsches Kunstinstitut, Frankfort a.M.

100

57-58. FOOT OPERATION (DETAILS, ACTUAL SIZE)

than in the Back Operation. Especial care has been given to representing the glittering high lights on the two bottles and the white jar in the right foreground. The light is quieter than in the preceding painting, and the tone is more expressly built upon grey and, in the figures, blue-grey. But the cavalier's sleeve is a dull yellow. The colours have been freely applied to the grey-brown ground. The painting must have been laid out in a neutral colour with fine nuances of tone, and only toward the end did the artist enliven and enrich it with these colour accents.

Among the paintings of the later years, only The Smokers can be dated on grounds of external evidence. The two panels in Frankfort can be grouped with it. But many works of high quality surely originating in the years between 1631 or 1632 and the end of 1637 do not form a real transitional stage between the groups of works here described as belonging to the early and the later Antwerp periods. The works of the intervening period fall into no clear sequence. There are several groups of related paintings, but only a few works clearly belonging among the early Antwerp production have a definite place in Brouwer's development.

It is to be expected in an artist's development that the last works will be the most freely painted, summarizing his personal, artistic handwriting, more suggesting than defining, spontaneous and loose, economical as to means, more and more abstracted from the exact, materialistic rendering of form—as we see in Rembrandt's development. But Brouwer died in his thirty-third year, and consequently it is inappropriate to speak of a style which is typical of old age or even of maturity. When Brouwer died, his contemporary Rembrandt had not yet begun the Night Watch; and Frans Hals at thirty-two had not even contemplated his

59. LOUSE CATCHER (ACTUAL SIZE)
Coll. J. C. H. Heldring, Oosterbeek (Holland)

first civic-guard piece. Thus Brouwer's work does not form a completed œuvre with the typical initial, middle and final periods. We shall have to discuss the remaining works in groups, so far as this is possible, and occasionally offer a suggestion about the place of a certain painting in the œuvre as a whole.

A few paintings show a connection with the sort of work which, like The Moerdijk Peasants, may have formed the transition between the Dutch and the Antwerp periods: such is the

102

60. THE QUARTET (ACTUAL SIZE)
Coll. J. C. H. Heldring, Oosterbeek (Holland)

103

original of the *Tooth Puller*, a copy of which, formerly in the Habich Collection, is now in the
Gallery in Karlsruhe (Bode 5; 24 × 32 cm.); and the original of the Quartet once in the
Kappel Collection, now on loan to the Museum in York from the Ettlinger Collection (Bode 2).
The latter is related in composition, moreover, to The Moerdijk Peasants. In the foreground
sits a young man, with a pipe in his right hand, looking back toward his three run-down com-
panions, who sit about a round table singing rather dejectedly. Is their condition not due more
to tobacco than to wine or beer? the quality of the painting in York rules out its being considered the original (p. 57). Bode looks on the panel with the three men from the van Gelder
Collection (Bode 43, here p. 92) as a pendant to the *Louse Catcher* (Bode 42; 18 × 16 cm.),
which came from the collection of Maurice Kann into that of J. C. H. Heldring in Oosterbeek,
Holland. The Louse Catcher is from a slightly later stage of Brouwer's development than the
former and is certainly of better quality. It is a strange scene: a man in a bluish-grey jacket
and yellow sleeve, with a white cap on his head, has taken a louse out of the long, lank hair of
a man bent over before him in an orange jacket, while a third fellow, wearing a brick-red cap
and a dark blue jacket, kills a louse between his fingers, with a grin on his face. The arrogant
expression of the barber is marvellous: he is going to burn his louse in the pipkin near him.
The background is kept a neutral grey-green. The artist has clearly produced the effect of
artificial light, shining from below to the left. It gives a fantastic character to the man's
grinning face. The painting is perhaps somewhat less finely finished than other Brouwers, and
somewhat awkward here and there, as in the hands; still there is no objection, particularly in
view of its very witty character, to regarding it as an original Brouwer.

Another slightly larger panel in the Heldring Collection also belongs to this period,
although of a different conception and execution: *The Quartet* (Bode 45; 22 × 18 cm.) It is
painted in a loose, fluid style and a cool tone, whereas the Louse Catcher is solid, precise and
warm. A figure which occurs repeatedly in the early Dutch works reappears here: the man
with raised arms in the background. But here this dark bat-like apparition dominates the
group with his broad gesture, holding in one hand a jug and in the other a glass of beer.
Another jug and a pipkin stand on the table; the man in front seems to be bawling a song from
the paper in his hand; behind him another man is bringing his greedy lips to his drink; his
neighbour, in a greenish jacket, while filling his pipe looks around at the exhorting apparition
with glass and jug. This unusual work is based on a light grey-brown tone. One is surprised
and exhilarated by the broad, spontaneous manner, the touch, the forceful and clear modelling;
more like Hals than Brouwer elsewhere shows himself, it is still a Brouwer through and through,
especially because of the demoniac significance of the bat-like figure, and because of the strong
light-accent formed by the yellow-white sleeve in the left foreground, continued in the singer's
light violet cap. It is a brilliant sketch, difficult to place because of its divergent character: al-

VI. Pig Slaughter
Collection J. C. H. Heldring, Oosterbeek (Holland)

though the connection with Hals, also evident in the grey colour, suggests the Dutch years, the complete freedom of treatment points to a somewhat more advanced development.

In complete contrast is *The Father's Disagreeable Task* in Dresden (Bode 48; 20 × 13 cm.), which has every claim to an early Antwerp date. It is probably a version by Brouwer of the subject Smell from a series of the Five Senses, a motif much painted in his day. This panel is as precise, firm and closed in treatment as the previous one is free, open and sketch-like. And here again fine nuances of colour play a role. The father wears a characteristic light blue beret and a rose-pink jacket; the little boy is wearing a brown jacket above his pink, plump behind which the father, his nose averted, is cleaning; behind them stands an old shrew.

Between two such extremes from a single period anything might be expected. In the two witty oval paintings in the Metropolitan Museum in New York, a *Man with a Bird* and a   61
Woman Fleaing a Dog (Bode 27 and 28; 18 × 14 cm.), both very sketchily and easily painted, (but   62
not with the broad touch of The Quartet in the Heldring Collection), the brushwork is precise, and the much stronger colours, on a brown ground tone, tend toward red in the man's hat and the woman's jacket. The man wears a warm brown jacket, the landscape is green in tone, the sky is blue and white; the woman wears a blue-green skirt, and the sky is grey. Yet the two panels do not have a colourful effect. We have placed them in this period on grounds, in the first place, of intuition, and also because the treatment of the landscape is freer and more personal than that, say, in the Fight over Cards in the Mauritshuis, and yet has not attained to the ethereal finesse and atmosphere of the late landscapes.

To this 'entourage' probably belongs the landscape which has recently come into the Heldring Collection, the *Pig Slaughter* in front of a farmstead (14 × 18 cm.), with a landscape on the   VI
left hand side that is reminiscent in many respects of the backgrounds in the oval pictures in New York. A pig is being butchered on a plank lying across a barrel; the four men, the woman and the child around it are small cloddish figures, loosely and almost casually sketched in. There is a touch of purplish red in their clothing, the only overpaint; the rest of the panel has been done in extremely thin, fluid, transparent paint. However much it appears to be concerned primarily with landscape and atmosphere, this scene too has the acute observation, the realistic and accordingly oppressive brutality and malevolence that Brouwer found in the world.

An artist of the first half of the seventeenth century can hardly be expected to express the sociological interest or the social compassion of our own times. But what then drove Brouwer to paint pictures which look like social accusations, when such a notion fits neither the spirit nor the thought-world of his period? Surely they were not meant to be humorous: that would have been too cruel; and the figures are too forlorn. Do they reveal Brouwer's view of humanity? Sometimes, and increasingly in his later work, he introduces a diabolic element into

61. MAN WITH A BIRD (ACTUAL SIZE)
The Metropolitan Museum of Art, New York (The Michael Friedsam Coll., 1931)

those heads. Does he, then, belong to the painters of obsession? Does it mean that he 'wrote down' such scenes because they took hold of his mind, although he would scarcely have been aware of the element of human dispossession and of pity for it? There must have been an inner necessity compelling Brouwer to portray a certain figure in exactly this and no other way. Cannot a man of the seventeenth century have felt dismay over human shortcomings? There is always the striking contrast between this distress and the extremely beautiful, sensitive form in which

106

62. Woman Fleaing a Dog (actual size)
The Metropolitan Museum of Art, New York (The Michael Friedsam Coll., 1931)

it is clothed. In any case it is clear that he does not make fun of his subjects even when they appear in the most impossible circumstances. He penetrates beyond the ridiculous; only mercy and pity remain. Consider that lamentable father, fulfilling his duty by his son's buttocks, driven as he is by the fierce hag of a woman: what a drama is depicted in his face, when looked at closely.

But Brouwer is not always so gloomy. In Munich there is the *Village Barber* busy with a VII

63-65. VILLAGE BARBER (DETAILS, ACTUAL SIZE)
Bayerische Staatsgemäldesammlungen, Munich

foot operation (Bode 54; Pinakothek[1] 561; 31×40 cm.), the brightest and most colourful of
the whole Munich series, and one of Brouwer's most richly furnished and sharply detailed
63 works. Because of its clear, entirely intelligible space, carefully and sensitively painted so that
64 the eye can easily scan it, this painting seems related to the late Dutch paintings and The
65 Moerdijk Peasants, but as a subsequent development from them. It is in sharp contrast to the
works just discussed, but since these were clearly sketches, they may well have been con-
temporaneous.

[1] The name of this Museum is now 'Bayerische Staatsgemäldesammlungen'. Since this famous collection is
known all over the world as 'Alte Pinakothek' we have kept this latter name in the text part of this book.

VII. Village Barber
Bayerische Staatsgemäldesammlungen, Munich

In this painting the stick in the right and the broom in the left foreground serve as anti-parallels to create space. The composition is in two halves, with a scene taking place in the left foreground, and a secondary one in the right background: the same arrangement as in the Antwerp Card Players, but here more consciously and more harmoniously carried out. This is a compositional scheme which, with a preference for having the foreground scene on the left, will recur; copyists often reproduced only the scene in the foreground.

The barber, who wears a warm brick-red hat (the colouristic centre of the picture) and a brown jacket, kneels over the foot of his patient, cutting into it with a sharp knife. The patient's face, beneath his shining cranium, twitches with pain. Behind them again stands the woman with a reserve lancet, ready to help; she leans on a sort of warming-stove; her attention is momentarily taken by a visitor pushing open the door. It is not the least of the charms of Brouwer's pictures that a story can always be found in them. He is the true realist who fascinates not by telling an out-of-the-way story, but rather by his manner of presentation. Why does she smile, not with hostility yet not without irony, toward the new patient? Does she anticipate some unpleasantness for him? Meanwhile in the right background the barber's colleague or assistant is occupied, examining something in the face or perhaps neck of the victim seated before him in a barrel chair; he pushes the head back with his left hand. Behind them the window admits a soft light through its diamond-shaped panes.

The importance of the profession of this village-surgeon is amply illustrated by the many instruments, the pots, jugs and bottles in which the light sparkles, by the skull and books on the shelf above the woman's head, and by the concentrated attention of the people to their work.

No other painting in Munich, perhaps no other Brouwer anywhere, equals this painting in clarity of presentation, in the development of the scene and details, except possibly the *Fight* VIII *over Cards*, also in Munich, one of the artist's larger paintings (Bode 55; Pinakothek 562; 33×49 cm.). This painting approaches the ideals of Dutch—emphatically not Flemish— 66 interior painting of later years: in clarity and solidity, in precise drawing and explicit representation of every form and object: for example the ear of the man on the left, the hand drawing the sword from its sheath, the jug on the bench in the foreground, the partition of planking against the rear wall with can and dishcloth hanging on it. This sort of clarity and purity in interior painting is to be found only in later Dutch works. The setting here is simple and compact: a corner of a dilapidated farm house. Four men, on the left, have been playing cards. A triangular stool has served as a table. The man on the right, to judge from his dress a stranger, and probably a soldier, sits on a basket turned upside down; the man opposite him sits on part of a barrel. But the stranger has cheated at cards, and the fat is in the fire. One of the players has jumped to his feet and takes hold of the stranger's hair with his left hand, raising a jug in his right with which to hit him on the head. A third man behind him tries to

66. FIGHT OVER CARDS (DETAIL, ACTUAL SIZE)
Bayerische Staatsgemäldesammlungen, Munich

hold him back. The culprit himself, his face twisted with rage and pain, is trying to draw his short sword. A fourth man—rather well-dressed, perhaps the farmer himself—is still seated, but in his right fist he holds a knife upright, and he reaches his left hand out threateningly. Finally there is an alarmed man bending over to enter the room through an undersized door-way in the upper right corner of the room.[1] Again, but this time less emphatically, the scheme of composition divides into a left foreground and a right background.

The figures are not brought so forcefully into the foreground; they are smaller in scale and less prominent. However dramatic and fascinating their action is, they have been worked into the space more harmoniously. The village barber's patient was still the bearer of a strong light-accent; we do not find it so here; apparently Brouwer moderated his light accents as he developed. The scene now is more evenly lit and coloured. The central figure, the card-sharper, wears a dark blue jacket and a pair of grey breeches; the man on the left—warmer and deeper—a purple hat, red-brown waistcoat and violet sleeves, and brown breeches; while the furious fellow in the middle is in blue-violet. The over-all tone is warm brown.

Brouwer has used almost the same fighting group again in *a similar triangular composition* in a painting in Dresden (Bode 57; 26.5 × 34 cm.). Having limited his attention to the three main figures, he similarly simplified the treatment of space and of details. This points to a later origin. The man on the left now wears a greenish grey hat, a steel-blue jacket and greenish breeches; the enraged fighter with the threatening jug wears a yellow-brown waistcoat from

(1) The perspective here is less than clear. What is the relationship between this door and the flight of stairs under it leading down into the room? The lintel of the doorway seems to be a part of the side wall, while the threshold belongs to the rear wall.

VIII. Fight over Cards
Bayerische Staatsgemäldesammlungen, Munich

which purple-brown sleeves protrude, and dark grey-blue breeches; while the third man is dressed in a peculiar light green. He has no sword this time: his face is deathly pale with terror; he turns to the right, his left arm forming one clearly marked side of the triangle. On the floor next to him lies his huge yellow hat. The painting of all the forms is emphatically solid and plastic.[1]) In the background three figures sit by the fireplace: an old couple, probably the innkeeper and his wife, with another man. The innkeeper has risen, not greatly perturbed by the tumult; he is an odd little man who appears with his villainous wife again and again in Brouwer's work. They seem to be a pair that made an impression on the painter at some time. He painted them repeatedly, the man in timid subjection to the old termagant; they are prominent in works which are clearly from the later years.

The *Messenger*, formerly in the Schloss Collection in Paris (Bode 111), belongs in the vicinity of these two Munich paintings: a peaceful scene which seems to anticipate similar pictures by Terborgh. Compared to the later paintings it is more fluent, more sketchily painted in places, and more focussed psychologically on the point of the story. The messenger with a sheet of paper in his hand and a cap with a feather on his head, does not bring pleasant tidings. The old man opposite him listens with compressed lips and raised eyebrows to the bad news; his arm holding the large jug hangs limpy. His wife, for Brouwer an unusually slender, dignified figure in her black dress and white kerchief, follows the alarming message, leaning across the back of the chair. Between them a young man listens seriously. Doubtless the information touches this very prosperous family of country people, possibly the family of a burgomaster or sheriff, deeply: it might concern the death of a son in battle.

Again we recognize the well-known compositional scheme of left foreground to right background, where two people are occupied in a corner. The foreground group is closed off in a striking manner by the two figures, placed one behind the other, with their backs to the right.

A *Tavern Scene* in the National Gallery in London, on loan from Sir Edmund Bacon (Bode 110; 48 × 76 cm.) exhibits a contrary scheme. This is the largest known painting by Brouwer, and one of the most important. The theme of the small painting in the Museum Bredius is here magnificently expanded.

The complicated construction of the composition, with its three centres, is peerless. In the smaller, left-hand part sits an extraordinary pair of lovers on a platform raised two steps above the floor. Sharply divided from this scene, three men sit talking pleasantly in the right foreground. They take no notice of the love-scene, although the one in the rear is turning his

67

68

IX

---

[1]) But La Chanson à Boire (Petit Palais in Paris) equally shows the same bareness and plasticity of forms. Might then the painting in Dresden be an indication that this work in Paris is yet an authentic one? The Drinking Song in the Bredius Museum, although it shows the same peculiarities, is too far off the Brouwer standard; just as the Tavern Scene in the National Gallery in London.

67. Tavern Scene
National Gallery, London (Coll. Sir Edmund Bacon, Bart.)

68. Tavern Scene (detail, actual size)

IX. TAVERN SCENE (DETAIL)

National Gallery, London (Collection Sir Edmund Bacon, Bart.)

69. DRAWING AFTER BROUWER'S TAVERN SCENE
Albertina, Vienna

head around. Two of the three have their backs to the couple. Behind this group is another of
three men, who show an exaggerated interest, with unavoidable antic comments.

Love-making is a very rare event in Brouwer's work. In this case the woman is not even
unattractive and so the man's desire for her is understandable. Her pose suggests a trollop.
Although she has grabbed him by his disordered hair, the expression of her face is only too
business-like regarding the man's hand intruding under her skirts; and although his face is
distorted with pain he is not about to give up his attempt. They were sitting drinking and the
tall beer-jug is rolling down the steps. Just above them is a man sticking his head through a
half-open shutter, enjoying the scene as much as the two leering men on the right and the
young man behind them who is stretching his head over their shoulders lest he miss any part of
the show. The contrast is striking between them and the two peaceable men in the foreground
and their turning comrade. The man on the right—who may be the innkeeper—, with a glass
in one hand and a jug in the other, sits chatting with a cavalier enjoying his pipe.

113

It is a somewhat wider, more luxurious space than is the rule in Brouwer's work: the mantle is substantial; the space on the left is less deep than that on the right; only the upper leaves of the window shutters are open.

There is no single colourful detail serving to bring the beholder's eye into the picture. Brouwer is striving for a more harmonious total impression. The lover on the left is in green-blue and grey, his companion wears a light yellow dress. The jerkin of the cavalier in the foreground is also yellow, but in warmer, browner hues and with brown sleeves; while the host wears a greyish shirt on top of a chestnut-coloured one, of which only the edge is visible, and a white cap. These colours are dominated by the warm brown tone.

The execution is not everywhere equal. Sometimes it is too easy, almost coarse; at other times there are details exhibiting an unexampled accuracy and subtlety: each of the faces is a case in point, as is the piece of paper with tobacco on the barrel to the right, or the towel hanging on the wall above it. The differences in execution testify to the freedom which the master can now permit himself and are guided by the importance of the different parts and by Brouwer's artistic whim: for him emphasis can also lie with the outward characteristics of the parts as well as with the total impression of the whole.[1]

34 A related scene, the *Tobacco Inn*, must have been an exceptionally popular one, to judge from the large number of extant examples, either of the entire picture or of the left half. Bode (3) reproduces the version formerly in the Arenberg Collection (31 × 40.5 cm.), while the best known is that in Dulwich College (31.5 × 41 cm.), and still a third is to be found in the Museum in Valenciennes. The latter is clearly inferior; between the other two no significant differences of quality are to be observed in the reproductions. Precisely because of its sound, cautious execution, the painting in Dulwich is not to be considered the original. (For further considerations see the discussion above, p. 59.) But the presentation and composition are typical of Brouwer. Again we have three centres of interest balanced against one another, although not so delicately as in the London tavern scene. In the left foreground is a group of seated men; on the right is one man standing by a wooden post which runs to the very top of the picture (a curious way to balance

(1) A drawing in the Albertina in Vienna (Bode 109; 14 × 18.3 cm.; not in Dresden, as Bode states) is regarded by Bode as an original Brouwer study for this composition. The differences between the drawing and the painting are not such as would have been introduced by a copyist, who would have had trouble in scaling the cavalier down to the insignificant peasant figure of the drawing, or in opening the lower leaves of the window so as to place a man in front of it, ignoring the business going on behind his back. More noticeable still is the dog, which in the
69 drawing is bounding towards the pair of lovers and forms a wedge in the composition between the right and the left sides: surely this was originally Brouwer's idea. The changes in the painting, including the omission of the dog, are improvements. Still the drawing is too poor to be an original Brouwer: consider, for example, the figure and particularly the head of the innkeeper. Probably there was another version of the painting. This would also explain how Brouwer, in the painting in London, which would then have been a variation on a previous work, was not consistently careful; he may even not have executed it all himself; at any rate he devoted his closest attention to those parts and details which were the particular point of this version.

X. INNKEEPER

Bayerische Staatsgemäldesammlungen, Munich

the composition); in the background in front of the hearth is a blurred group of figures seen indistinctly, mostly from the back. There is not present here the dynamic relationship between these three elements that one observes in the London painting, a fact which suggests a somewhat later, more mature origin for the latter.[1]

The tobacco in use here is producing grave narcotic effects: certainly it is the 'belladonna'-hemp mixture that was to be encountered in secret, forbidden Flemish taverns. The cavalier-like smoker on the left of the Dulwich painting, who sits with his fist on his thigh enjoying himself with a certain bravado, is a forerunner of the smoker in New York, and might even be a somewhat earlier self-portrait.

A fat *Innkeeper* enthroned in a barrel-chair on a platform is the principal subject of a picture X in Munich (Bode 67; 31 × 24 cm.). Seated in the left foreground, he faces toward the space of the inn room; but he is sound asleep and his contact with the scene is broken. On the right, deep in the background and shrouded in tone, Brouwer has assembled a very unsavoury company. Clearly it is drink which in this case has the group round the table in its devastating clutches. One of the revellers lies vomiting on the floor, to the delectation of the pigs that are playing the part of scavengers. Understandably one of the group is on his way out of the room. Of the six remaining people, two or three seem to be women, but no less drunk for that. The imposing, beautifully painted head of a boar drinking out of a trough occupies the right foreground. Is he meant to symbolize the entire situation? An owl is sitting on the open shutter. All is painted with the perspicacious taste of the sophisticated lover of the beautiful and the essential in form and colour. There is no single strong note of colour save the hat on the chair-back, which is a sober purple-red. The back of the sleeping man in the background is a dull steel-blue. The scene is painted in the very finest nuances of brown tones, with some delightful, scintillating light-points, such as in the copper pan in the foreground. The picture is emphatically static; it generates a pleasant tranquillity which even the drinkers in their shadowy corner in the rear do not break into.

The contrast, however, must remain, because it gives a point to the innkeeper's placid rest. One can regard it as something of a parable, executed in the spirit of that emblem-loving period; a certain moralizing or at least contemplative element is not foreign to Brouwer. But

[1] In the Prado in Madrid there are two scenes of similar format (33 × 55 cm.): neither can be regarded as an original, but both are related to the scene under discussion, particularly the one with a group on the left which is in part the same as the corresponding group in the Dulwich picture. (The post dividing the space is absent in both Madrid pictures). The other shows on the right a group of people singing by a flaming fire and on the left a large and probably beautifully painted still life, with an emphatic composition, which, although unlike Brouwer, is reminiscent of works of the Rotterdam School (Sorgh, for example). There were repeated contacts between Antwerp and Rotterdam painters in the seventeenth century. In yet another painting—one in the collection of Lord Ellesmere in Edinburgh—(see above, p. 61; there still considered to be a Brouwer) the group of singers becomes a composition in itself.

this literary element is so discreetly worked into his compositions that they are overlooked by the modern beholder—although his contemporaries would have noticed and appreciated them. They are as essential to the taste of the seventeenth century as they are exceptional to our own.

This Brouwer, depicted by himself and imagined by us as not lacking in swagger—this Brouwer is essentially discrete, at least in his art, and becomes increasingly so with time. His preference for the small and the very small picture, and the ever increasing dominance of tone in his pictures bear this out. His pictures do not seize the beholder's attention. One walks past them in the great museums. But as soon as one has noticed them, such paintings as this one of the sleeping inn-keeper afford wonderful experiences. How fascinating is the delicacy and beauty of the entire picture, with its exquisite, still colour scheme, its lovely transparent tone, the pointed care with which the still-life is painted. How sensitively rendered is the rotund inn-keeper, his head fallen forward, the jug in his relaxed left hand and a rough stick in the other. The effect of deep rest in the warm mid-day beneath the open window is tellingly expressed—and then one comes upon the raw scene, like something from an entirely different world, discreetly tucked away in the background. Is the point to be found in the sharp contrast between these two scenes, or does the background scene serve merely to set off the imperturbability of utter rest? Brouwer only holds the scene before us without overt comment; but clearly he expects the beholder to let his thoughts linger over its meaning.

He is not always so. As a rule, and always in the earlier works, we find no devices for introducing ideas of a speculative nature. But perhaps they escape us, because we are not initiated into these trains of thought.

In this vein there are two apparently uncomplicated gaming scenes also in the Munich Pina-
70 kothek: the *Card Players* (Bode 107; 24.5 × 34.5 cm.; Pin. 2108) and *Soldiers Gambling* (Bode 106; 35 × 46 cm.; Pin. 242): both compositions are strikingly simple, with even grey walls as backgrounds, comparatively large figures in almost empty space and remarkably few subsidiary details. This does not reflect a want of industry, but the fact that the artist wished to concentrate even more than ever on the beautiful, carefully and strongly painted figures. In the Soldiers Gambling there are some undistinguished old people by the side door in the background, and in the foreground is a white earthenware jug that is, taken by itself, a small marvel of painting. Three picturesquely clothed men, obviously soldiers, sit dicing around a small table; a fourth, perhaps the innkeeper, looks on with interest. How cleverly the painter has put the two curious tall hats to use in the composition. And how marvellously the four faces are painted, each so distinctive in its role that one can weave a story about the scene. The odds are against the elegant young man in the foreground, perhaps an officer; he is being taken in by the other two. He affords the light grey-blue accent in this composition, again based on warm brown. Brouwer has given close attention to painting the apparently inessential details, such as the

70. SOLDIERS GAMBLING
Bayerische Staatsgemäldesammlungen, Munich

woven pattern in the blue sleeve and the hilt of the sword and the buttons on the breeches of this foreground figure; or similar particulars, such as the fine white cuffs and collar, in the costume of the man in brown opposite him. Apparently the latter has just risen for what is to be the decisive throw: the eyes of the man on his left flash with excited expectation.

In the other picture, the Card Players, two soldiers sit in an even barer inn; one is on a chair, the other straddles a long bench which also serves as a card-table. Two peasants watch, 71 as the man on the left triumphantly puts his cards down on the bench; but his opponent still 72 has something in reserve. He chuckles behind his cards, his huge hat pushed half-way down 73 his forehead. What a splendid figure! How enchantingly this moment in the game has been captured!

The man's enormous hat is pale purple, his jacket grey-blue; the man on the left wears much darker blue. There are no other colours in this closed composition, in which the hats function

117

71. CARD PLAYERS
Bayerische Staatsgemäldesammlungen, Munich

as a part of the circular form of the figure group. The master has left nothing to chance.

These two works are not far from the execution, characterization and spirit of the Foot Operation in Frankfort. But, as we have already noted, it is not possible to construct a strict chronological order for these Antwerp works. Brouwer, an artist in love with his art, steadily altered his technique as he thought each separate case required; even these two paintings are differently treated. He took pleasure in finding for each isolated artistic problem a new solution. And yet he consistently saw the separate problems subordinate to the whole: the appropriateness of characterization, both of situations and of persons; the sharp, decisive representation of outward forms; the purity and beauty of the relations in tone and colour, in space and form. Brouwer never loses sight of the tension between these components; all are equally important to him, yet he likes to give emphasis on one occasion to this, on another occasion to that element.

Here these works have been arranged in a loose sequence, with the particular object

118

72. SOLDIERS GAMBLING
(DETAIL, ACTUAL SIZE)

73. CARD PLAYERS
(DETAIL, ACTUAL SIZE)

furnishing a bridge between the closed, plastic representations such as the Foot Operation in Munich, and the much freer treatment—although at the same time concentrated and exquisite—to be found in The Smokers in New York.

These two paintings in Munich would appear to be not far from the end of this sequence. Yet there are still other works, some differently treated, which are difficult to place. One must remember that all of these works originated in a period of not more than five years. One such is the *Drinking Company* in Munich (Bode 108; 36 × 27 cm.; Pin. 2063); it seems to belong 74 close to the two foregoing pictures but is without their detail and extreme finesse of execution. In breadth of treatment and undetailed surroundings it approaches the two surgeon-scenes in Frankfort; the broad, effectively painted still life on the table is treated altogether in the manner of the Back Operation.

The intense blue back of the man seated in the foreground provides the dominant note of colour: it is not so much contrasted to the much darker, almost violet-blue of the other

119

costumes and the hats of both the innkeeper and the figure in blue, as it is the strongest force near them. Once again the expressions have been wonderfully captured with a striking variation in technique between the painting of the host's face and that of the jolly drinker holding the enormous glass. The bare room and massive door on the right have been handled in great sweeping planes.

The same comparatively bare space, monumentalityc and clearly ordered simplicity are also elements of the engaging *Sleeping Man* in the Wallace Collection (Bode 68; 36 × 27 cm.). The big gawky young man sitting in front of the crude plank partition is also painted in shades of dull purple (breeches), brown (leggings) and violet (jacket), the colours which Brouwer preferred. Deep in the tone of the background on the left are a few figures. There are other, wider versions of this picture in which the background is more extensively developed. But since Brouwer's intention here seems to have been to monumentalize the subject of sleeping off a drunk, one can assume that in this case not the more extensive but the more limited composition is the original. Note the blissful smile on the young man's face.

It is the same with the picture from the Wellington Collection in Apsley House in London: 75 *Two Cavaliers*, who are occupied in a tobacco-inn with enjoying their narcotic pipes (Bode 114).[1] 76 It is true that the painting of the clothing has become broader, even more nonchalant than is Brouwer's custom, but this is also the case in The Smokers in New York and the Back Operation in Frankfort. The colour in these clothes, although subdued, is exceptionally crisp and subtle. The large figure in the foreground wears a yellow waistcoat with striking white sleeves protruding from it, and a pair of violet breeches. The other cavalier, leaning back heavily, wears a greenish violet jacket over grey-blue breeches. A warm red accent is provided by the hat on the back of the chair to the left. If these clothes, as planes of colour, are treated somewhat broadly, not so the men's hands and faces. Is the man in the foreground, lighting his long pipe from a stick of wood again a self-portrait? Between the two smokers is a young man watching with close attention. The man on the left has just begun to smoke, whereas his comrade on the right is already under the influence of this vicious pleasure: leaning back in his chair he gazes at distant visions. No less impressive is the third principal figure, the innkeeper's wife in the background, who is bringing another jug, and in passing offers an ironic commentary to a witch-like old woman looking in through a window. Her gestures suggest that business is good.

(1) There are repetitions of this scene in, among other places, Budapest, Vienna and the Liechtenstein Collection. The qualities of the example in London, the beautifully painted faces, the delicate shading of colour, make it probable that this one is the original; but the example in the Liechtenstein Collection also stands a chance. The latter has, in some respects, attractive qualities, such as the looser, more spontaneous style, which in this later period is perhaps more like Brouwer. There are a few small differences. The brass nail heads in the chair-back are missing in the Liechtenstein picture. Is this to be put down to the indolence of the imitator, or, on the contrary, did the possible copyist responsible for the London painting wish to improve on the original?

74. DRINKING COMPANY

Bayerische Staatsgemäldesammlungen, Munich

121

75. TWO CAVALIERS
Wellington Museum, Apsley House, London

122

76. TWO CAVALIERS (DETAIL, ACTUAL SIZE)

Did the painter himself put the letters 'BROU' on the bench at the right? In any case, they do not lie.

Again the bleakness of the space indicated focuses attention on the people and their activities, on the actual motif of the painting, if not indeed on the technique itself. This economy of means, contrasted to the unrelaxed accuracy and elaboration of the Foot Operation in Munich, should be regarded as a later stage in Brouwer's development. Is this omission of subordinate details related to a disordered way of life which left Brouwer increasingly less time to devote to his work? His large tavern-debts are established fact. Is the image shifting to that of a less conscientious artist, less absorbed in his work? Whether or no, his craftsmanship remains as skilled, certain and disciplined as ever. Still, are certain weaknesses in the paintings of his later years, such as the left cheek of the smoker in New York, to be regarded as lapses? If so, they would have been exceptional and limited in extent—and why did he not correct them in a more favourable moment? The forceful precision, the immediate expressive possibilities and the colouristic distinctions of the late paintings testify to an artistry in no way enfeebled—unless one interpret the slightly darker tonality of the New York painting as evidence of a lack of ability? The later stage reflects a more fluent, a broader but a less penetrating technique, similar to the technique of his contemporary, Rembrandt's, in the same years (about 1635–1640). This great breadth and freedom, along with a certain indifference toward

123

77. LUTE PLAYER

Victoria and Albert Museum (Ionides Collection), London

124

78. Peasants and Soldiers Playing Cards

Bayerische Staatsgemäldesammlungen, Munich

finical detail, is entirely in agreement with the general development of Netherlands art in these years.

Also in London, in the Victoria and Albert Museum, hangs a painting which shows the contrasts in Brouwer's craftsmanship at this time perhaps more clearly: the *Lute Player* (Ionides Collection; Bode 105; 36.2 × 28.7 cm.). It is jauntily painted; the cat on the left is curiously awkward and the painting of the floor behind it is careless. The luteplayer's head is put in in a few strokes, yet how splendidly inimitable is his expression, and how delightful is the laughing woman behind the bowl of mussels on the table. Note such captivating details as the two mussel shells on the floor, or the smoking candle in the copper sconce, or the small still life on the shelf against the wall, which includes a warm-red pot, among other things. This is an instance of Brouwer's ability suddenly to put a still life, painted with great tenderness and sensitivity, in the midst of a scene otherwise treated in an extremely sketchy manner. His artistic temperament was capricious.

77

125

One is struck by the colourfulness and the unusually light tone of this painting. There is a heavy yellow varnish over the pigment, but this does not entirely account for the decidedly yellow tone of the floor and background. The man is dressed in a light purple outfit and yellow-brown shoes; the woman, again, is in green-blue: the typical Brouwer colour-scheme. This new broad and fluid, sometimes even cursory manner need not be a consequence of weakness or diminishing powers of concentration; it is an application of a known artistic method used in a brilliant fashion to dynamize a scene, ultimately leading to Goya-like effects of demoniac, visionary power, and to the superbly lambent atmospheric qualities of his late landscapes.

There is in Munich (Bode 60; 33 × 43 cm.; Pin. 218) a larger composition of *Peasants and*
78 *Soldiers Playing Cards* in a tavern. A distinct, fully plastic representation, as in the large black-blue and brown jugs in the foreground or the low bench on the left and the big pot on it, alternates with a broad, suggestive style which is here better controlled than in the Lute Player; the modelling is stronger and the painting is less fluid. Three excited ruffians are looking on as two other men play cards: one, a peasant with cherry-red breeches and a white-grey jacket; the other, a soldier in contrasting green. On the rough table lies an utterly threadbare, deep blue cloth. In the left hand corner two men sit quarrelling fiercely. These seven figures form a distinctly closed group, from which only the card-playing peasant on the right remains somewhat apart. Tension and action are keenly depicted; the space is exceptionally bare and empty. The innkeeper and his wife,—the same curious old couple previously noticed,—sketchily indicated are talking by the fire-place in the right background. Suddenly the artist's attention has fixed on the window-shutter in the top left corner: the old boards are beautifully painted, with the chalk score-marks and a stick figure drawn on. All in all a gifted, fascinating caprice of contrasting effects: sometimes concentrated and thorough, sometimes loose and relaxed.

79   Bode 4: *Tobacco Inn*: Six men are sitting together in a bare room, under the influence of tobacco, each in his own world; a seventh, apparently very drunk, is coming in (35 × 26 cm.; Pin. 2062). The spiritual isolation of each of the six is reflected in the loose, open composition. It is a pattern-card of reactions to the pernicious 'belladonna'.

The strongest colour accent is the deep brick-red hat of the man in the foreground wearing a blue-grey jacket and olive-green breeches; the bench in the foreground with a white cloth, a jug and a loaf of bread also catches the eye. The rest is in a warm tone, in which shades of purple and violet dominate.

XI   In the *Tobacco Inn* in the Louvre (Bode 31; 20 × 28 cm.) Brouwer has attempted still more emphatically to work with a single powerful and warm colour accent. Here the whole painting seems to be composed around the warm yellow of the breeches and the pale purple of the waistcoat and, between these two, the salient white shirt worn by the man in the foreground sitting sprawled over the table. In this way Brouwer is able to build this figure, enlarged and

79. TOBACCO INN
Bayerische Staatsgemäldesammlungen, Munich

127

80. Tobacco Inn (detail, actual size)
Musée du Louvre, Paris

exceptionally plastic, into the central motif; this triad of colours is enlivened by the red laces in waistcoat and breeches, and the red beret—colour effects such as Vermeer sought after. The composition is so well-knit that one is surprised to find that no fewer than nine figures, including one or two children, are merged into this small, compact group. Yet at the same time it is an orgy in isolation: the three principal figures are no longer aware of each other. The one in front has sunk into a deep sleep. What types the other two are! A death's head is conjured up by the horrible face of the man with the dark cap pulled down over his eyes, holding his pipe in the pipkin. A new and arresting painting technique has been employed here: a sort of angular, gruff touch, modelling with strong light-and-dark contrasts, in very short strokes, and with a very solid portrayal of form. There is an immeasurable distance between this technique and the academically correct style of the Smokers in Kassel, and the painter has gained accordingly in expressive power. One is taken aback as when confronted with a head by Goya—more and more affinities with the great demoniac Spaniard appear; there is no mockery or irony, only revelation and tragedy. The sparsely furnished surroundings, constructed in solid, impenetrable forms, are a suitable setting. Is the queer man dressed in black, who looks up, completely lost in a trance, a religious? The clergy in Flanders strongly condemned these narcotics . . . do we here see another analogy with Goya?

The painting of the highly coloured back and legs in the foreground is beautiful, exceptionally strong and thoroughly finished. All Brouwer's delight in painting is expressed in the treatment of this man; once the numbness of his sleep has been expressed, there is little more story to tell. The fondly embracing couple to the right—what a strange place, this, for lovemaking—is of decidedly secondary importance, but is none the less painted with sturdy, vigorous plasticity, as are the two men and two children standing outside of the main action by the hearth.

80

128

XI. Tobacco Inn
Musée du Louvre, Paris

81. YOUNG MAN WITH A MUG (ACTUAL SIZE)
Staedelsches Kunstinstitut, Frankfort a.M.

This is one of Brouwer's most mature creations, belonging both spiritually and artistically to his later years.

A new means of expression appears here in the treatment of the man holding his pipe in the pipkin. There are other paintings in which a somewhat similar—yet not identical— manner appears: Brouwer varies constantly.

The oval painting in Frankfort of a *Young Man with a Mug* dressed in clothing of warm 81 colours, may belong in this category: it is wonderfully strong and sound, yet sketch-like. How imaginatively the thoroughly depraved face and unkempt locks are portrayed. Behind him, indicated by a few brush strokes, is a rowdy company seated around a table. The same peculiar little man already observed elsewhere appears again here as innkeeper (Bode 30; 13 × 18 cm.).

There is a second *Fight Scene* in Munich, this time situated around a barrel in a tavern 82 (Bode 65; 30 × 25 cm.; Pin. 861). This may have originated at the same time as the Card Players in the same museum (78, see above p. 126), for the same shutter appears in the upper left-hand corner—yet not identically painted. The master never repeats himself

129

82. FIGHT SCENE

Bayerische Staatsgemäldesammlungen, Munich

130

83. FIVE MEN FIGHTING
Bayerische Staatsgemäldesammlungen, Munich

84. FIVE MEN FIGHTING (DETAIL, ACTUAL SIZE)

131

85. Two Peasants Fighting (actual size)
Bayerische Staatsgemäldesammlungen, Munich

slavishly! Neither the stick-figure nor the splintered places are precisely the same. Still it is the same shutter, as appears from the lighter board at the left and the triangular shadow above. It is noteworthy that the painter should repeat this one element, yet in a different interior, smaller and, although there is a shelf with pots against the rear wall, generally barer. By means of this smallness the space is narrowed to contain the exceptionally compressed, closed composition—as static in contour as it is dynamic in content. A furious scoundrel—what a face, what a fierce eye!—is beating his opponent's head against the top of a barrel; the latter shrieks with pain, but a woman is running to his assistance. The construction of the heads brings to mind the head of the man in the previous picture, and here too the painting is robust, striking, simple and plastic. The right background, however, is somewhat carelessly brushed in,

132

86. Two Peasants Fighting (detail, twice actual size)

with the recurrent freakish little man, now very dirty, in the corner. (Such figures as this one are often feebly painted: did Brouwer have an assistant?) On the other hand, the iron ring on the shutter is a masterpiece of skilful painting.

In contrast to the painting in the Louvre, there is no single prominent colour. The light ruffian wears a yellow-grey jacket and a pair of dun purplish breeches, the same colours as the figure seen from the rear in the Paris picture, but much less striking.

An even rowdier scene is another in Munich showing *Five Men Fighting* (Bode 44; 23 × 31 cm.; Pin. 2050). Three of them are around a barrel; the one on the right, drawing a short sword, has been forced to his knees by the enraged fellow behind him who has him by the head; the third man, on the left, seems to be coming to his rescue. This latter man is wearing the same pale colours: a yellow-white jacket, light violet breeches and a soft raspberry-coloured cap; the man with the sword has a faded light sleeve. This delicate colour-composition is in striking contrast to the bestiality of the scene. Behind this first group there is a man with a cudgel chasing another man, who is screeching, out of the door. In the right background the scruffy little man reappears, this time with an enormous jug in his arms; he is at the foot of four steps leading to a door, through which his wife shouts something after him. Again this corner of the painting has been artistically neglected; but this is not the case with the familiar post standing in the foreground, with a bowl and a cloth hanging on it. The painter's attention has concentrated on the old, weathered wood. The reasonable conclusion

133

from these paintings is that the brilliant Brouwer systematically applies ever more economical means. Perhaps he was beginning to lack both the desire and the self-control required to devote his full attention to subsidiary details. Not far away were the examples of Rubens and van Dyck, who had assistants specializing in certain types of subsidiary work.

The last and most concentrated of the fight scenes in Munich is a very small panel with just two half-figures next to a barrel with a jug on it: the *Two Peasants Fighting* (Bode 56; 15.5 × 14 cm.; Pin. 2112). It may, indeed, be the last of this entire series, perhaps one of Brouwer's last paintings. The small surface is full of surprises, especially that of the piquant contrast between treatment and subject, between the colour-scheme and the atmosphere of the moment. One of the men has jumped up and jabs toward his opponent's head; the second, however, striking out behind, has already landed a fierce blow on the other's jaw: the disordered, enraged face of the first man more than ever foreshadows Goya.

It is always dangerous to subject violent motion to the fixity of a visual rendering. The film has taught us that in the exact reproduction, in the rigidity of the single fixed image the illusion of motion vanishes. Statues of men mounted on prancing horses are for this reason always disappointing, regardless of how well they are executed. Such artists as Delacroix and Degas appear to have felt this: by the conscious use of artistic tricks they preserved the suggestion of motion. Brouwer sought this solution primarily in using compositional schemes with forceful, dynamic channels of motion. This appears clearly in the painting under discussion, and its effect is reinforced by the violent expressions.

After all this, does one still have any attention left for considering the colour? Brouwer did: the colour-treatment here is so subtle that it brings to mind the calm, gentle scenes of Terborgh. The seated man wears a large yellow felt hat, a warm-green jacket and light yellow breeches; his assailant has on a violet-grey jacket with burgundy-red cuffs. The coral-red cord across the white split in the green waistcoat and trousers again is a particular colouristic refinement.

With this painting we have come perhaps to the end of one of Brouwer's different possible lines of development. Apparently the question of a falling off is not pertinent. The Two Peasants Fighting, probably of a later date than The Smokers in New York, can be regarded all in all as a more faultless painting than the latter: but since it is simpler it offered fewer opportunities for missteps than did the larger, more complicated painting. The Smokers does not have the warm, satisfying colour-appeal of the fight-scene, but as I suggested before, a cleaning would probably bring surprising results. And the artist's attention goes truly deeper, in The Smokers, achieving greater variation of expression and the means of expression than in the small Munich action snap-shot.

There remain still a few of the works in Munich to be considered. Three of them appear to

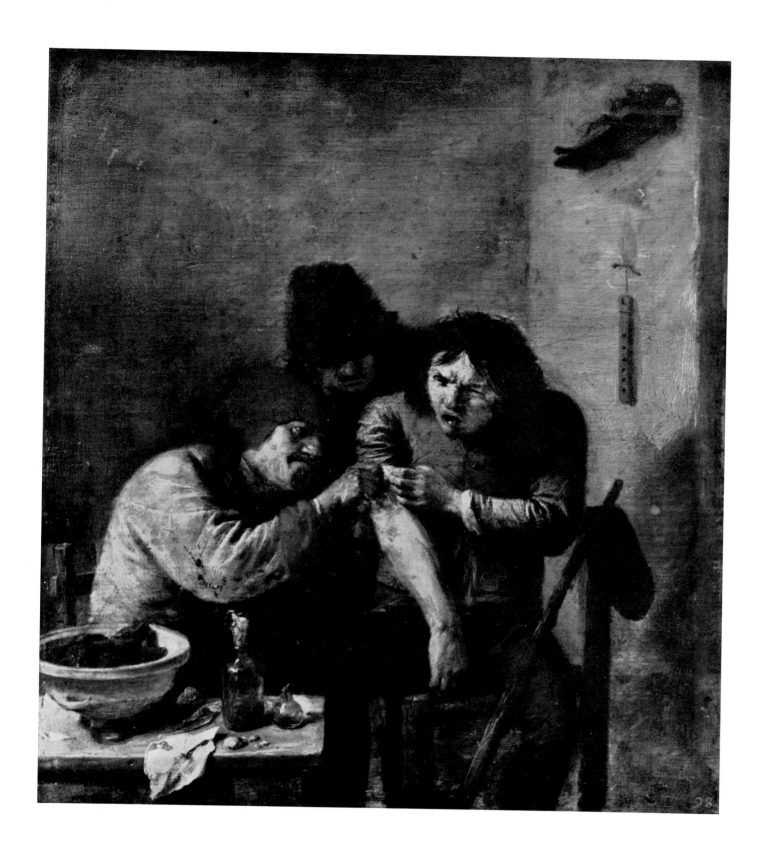

87. Touch

Bayerische Staatsgemäldesammlungen, Munich

135

88. Taste
Bayerische Staatsgemäldesammlungen, Munich

136

89. Taste (detail, twice actual size)

belong together as images of touch, hearing and taste. I suggested that the much earlier painting of the Father's Unpleasant Task also, as a representation of Smell, belongs to another series of the Five Senses. Brouwer does not appear to have been much taken by this stale theme· Perhaps the pictures were commissioned by one of his creditors, who would thus have got five paintings at once. Such decoration would certainly have been appropriate in a tavern.

Touch (Bode 70; 23 × 20 cm.; Pin. 581): three half-figures are organized in a closed composition. A surgeon is letting blood from the bare arm of a man with a markedly pained expression. The third man, only sketched in, watches over the patient's shoulder. The still life in the foreground, consisting of a bowl, some bottles, a piece of cloth and miscellaneous small objects is again very perceptively rendered. The colour is in moderated shades: a warm brick-red hat and cuffs, with a purple-violet jacket for the surgeon; the patient in shades of blue with touches of yellow-brown. The painting of the background is strong.

87

90. HEARING
Bayerische Staatsgemäldesammlungen, Munich

91. SMELL

Bayerische Staatsgemäldesammlungen, Munich

139

88 *Taste* (or perhaps *Smell*; Bode 71; 23 × 20 cm.; Pin. 626): again there are three half-figures.

89 Each is depicted in a different phase of the smoking ritual: one fills his pipe, the second lights it and the third exhales the smoke. The last is well on the way to being stupified: what expression there is in the painting of this head, of the gruesome, half-witted, dazed face. The group is less compactly constructed than the preceding one, the setting is bare, the entire treatment thin and sketchy, the colours are beautiful, but not so warm and striking.

90 *Hearing* (Bode 69; 24 × 20 cm.; Pin. 629) is a more complicated composition of five figures. The four in the background are gathered round the hearth singing: the treatment is almost caricature-like, fluid and sketchy and even tending, in the case of the standing man, to carelessness. It seems as if another hand has been active here. But the violinist in the foreground, seated on a low half-barrel, may be the work of Brouwer. He wears a red hat, dark green jacket and yellow breeches (on rather short legs). His laughing face with one eye shut is engaging.

91 *Smell* may be the subject of the sketchy scene of two peasants smoking, but if so it belongs to another series (Bode 32; 21 × 19 cm.; Pin. 2095). The foremost man sits with a jug in one hand and a pipe in the other, blowing out smoke in a dazed manner; he wears a loose-fitting olive-green jacket and violet breeches. Behind him a man in grey is lighting a lunt in the fire. Is this careless sketch by Brouwer himself? The smoker's vacant face, so lacking the evidences of Brouwer's penetrating observations, does not support the attribution.

Related to this is a singular composition showing a *Smoker* seated on a flimsy three-legged stool. With one foot on a bench, he leans far back, lost in his visions. On his knee he holds a beer jug. In the background a little man relieves himself, standing with his back to the beholder. Altogether an empty composition, and not an original Brouwer, but perhaps an idea which originated with Brouwer. (Formerly in the Maurice Kann Collection; subsequently in the hands of the art dealer Schäffer in New York; 24 × 19 cm.)

There are a number of paintings (some occurring in several similar versions) in which the entire picture is focussed on a single smoker. Such is the *Man in a White Jacket* (formerly in the Goudstikker Collection; Bode 72; 21 × 15.5 cm.), which looks like a repetition of the Taste in Munich, already discussed. The jacket hanging loosely outside the breeches is not very successful, and even less so is the manner of painting: it is difficult to regard it as an original Brouwer. But the notable composition, in which a second man appears opposite the first in a nebulous tone as in a vision, may derive from Brouwer.

92 The *Smoker* wearing a brown cap, violet-grey jacket and green breeches in the Rijksmuseum, Amsterdam (29.5 × 21 cm.) is a much better and a more important picture. He sits with his left leg stretched out on a block of stone and, holding a pipe in his raised right hand, exhales smoke. Again the hallucinating effects of the foul mixture are evident. Peculiar, although beautiful as a warm colour-note, is the little brown-red man entering the room in

92. SMOKER
Rijksmuseum, Amsterdam

the right background, still doing up his breeches. Another man, in a grey cocked hat and blue sleeve, sits sleeping behind the smoker. Because of its deep, warm colour, and even more because of the typing and portrayal of the fellow in the background, this picture is surely to be considered a late work.

93. Young Man Sitting on the Floor
Hammer Collection, U.S.A.

A small panel in Berlin-Dahlem (19 × 15 cm.) also depicts a *Smoker Seated in a Decrepit Barrel-chair*, a beer-pot in one hand and a pipe in the other. The treatment is very sketchy, with the red of the fire as the only touch of colour: a fine small work, with a good claim to being an original.

The oval painting which came into the Hammer Collection in the United States from
93 the Larsen-Menzel Collection (Wassenaar, Holland; 13.5 × 18 cm.) shows a *Young Man Sitting on the Floor*, dejectedly asleep; his head is leaning against a low wall, there is a jug between his knees, and his black dog is near him. In the background there is that silly little old man again, this time seated in the privy with the door wide open. An original? It is difficult to say, but if so, surely only an off-hand sketch, although painted strongly and with decision.

The versatility of the master within his relatively small œuvre is notable. In addition to this mixed procession of scenes, varying in content but particularly in the spirit of their artistic conception and the problems they set out to solve, there still remain works that are difficult to include with those already discussed (not to mention the country-scenes, which will be treated separately).

94. FIGHT SCENE
The Metropolitan Museum of Art, New York, (The Michael Friedsam Coll., 1931)

There are several instances of a *Fight Scene* with three half-figures moved slightly to the left of the picture, in front of an unspecified background. Two men have fallen out over dice: the figure in the middle has raised aloft a jug to deal a blow to the man on the right; the figure on the left is trying to restrain the first. The different copies, in the Museum in Dresden, in the 94 Metropolitan Museum in New York, in the Museum in Lyons, among others, appear to be similar in quality. The Dresden picture (Bode 62; 22.5 × 17 cm.) is, like the others, kept to a dark tone composed of violet, brown-purple and green-blue, the only white high-lights being the shirt

143

95. Two Smokers
Coll. F. F. Madan Esq., London

collars and-cuffs. The imposing composition, a triangle with a sharp, high apex, is full of the dynamic movement of violent fighting; one can think of this composition as belonging in the vicinity of the late fight-scene in Munich.

95   The *Two Smokers* in the Madan Collection in London (22.8×19 cm.) is reminiscent of the painting just discussed, in its high format and in its manner. It, too, shows a closed group in the left half of the panel with one man standing behind a second who has fallen asleep over a keg. The strange, drunkenly distorted face of the standing man is beautifully painted in a

96. THE CONTRACT (ACTUAL SIZE)
Coll. J. C. H. Heldring, Oosterbeek (Holland)

rather flaky, broad touch. The base tone of the background is yellowish with fine original overpainting of green-grey. The figures are brown, with somewhat darker violet tones in the sleeping man.

Connected with this is the composition of *Four Men Round a Table* with a bit of herring, a loaf of bread and a knife. On the far right sits a man with a large cocked hat. All four are far from sober; the standing man seems to be on the point of vomiting (Bode 46; formerly in the Stokvis Collection in Brussels). The representation falls short of the surprising, convincing revelation that characterizes Brouwer. The manner of painting, in small, hatched brush-strokes, suggests an imitator rather than a copyist, for a copyist would not, for one thing, have drawn the arm with the glass so badly.

To the Heldring Collection belongs *The Contract* (14.5 × 11.5 cm.), a small, spirited scene 96

97. UNIDENTIFIED PAINTER, PEASANT QUARTET
Bayerische Staatsgemäldesammlungen, Munich

which shows a man with a sly, amused expression, writing what two other men are concocting from some sort of document which they hold before them. This composition is, in its acute characterization and in such details as the small still life on the shelf against the wall, typical of Brouwer, and the triangular composition belongs with the works just discussed.

The inventory of the Alte Pinakothek in Munich includes three Brouwers not yet discussed here; two of these have already been demoted by the directors themselves: the *Innkeeper and his Wife Sampling Wine* (Bode 115; 39 × 58 cm.; Pin. 1281; at present in the Museum in Regensburg) and a *Tavern Interior* showing a man standing with his back to the hearth (32 × 25 cm.; placed in the Museum at Aschaffenburg). The third is the largest among the 97 Munich Brouwers: the *Peasant Quartet* (Bode 104; 43 × 52 cm.; Pin. 109) is a beautifully and carefully painted work in a fine grey tone, but it is not in Brouwer's manner. It may very well date from after Brouwer's death, and even brings to mind the eighteenth-century English painter Morland. Consider the engaging dog with pups in the right foreground, which is

146

particularly reminiscent of this English master (Brouwer would have preferred a pig here!). The mother with her child by the hearth is similarly outside Brouwer's sphere—unless at the end of his life he chose to go in for charming domestic scenes.

From these Antwerp years there are, apparently spread over the entire period, a number of small paintings, without action, each of only a single figure; some are half-lengths, others just head-and-shoulders. They are free, more or less portrait-like studies of character or expression, and parables. By 'parables' I mean representations of abstract ideas such as the Seven Deadly Sins or the Five Senses: emblems, accordingly—a type of subject which was still very popular in the Netherlands in Brouwer's time. Thus the scene in Dresden of the Father's Unpleasant Task already discussed was probably a representation of Smell and some compositions in Munich might supposedly represent the Senses.

The ovals in New York of the man with a bird and the woman with a dog in her arms may belong to this class of paintings, although dating from the Dutch period. They are not pendants, since they both face in the same direction; they may have belonged to a larger series, but what conception they illustrate is not clear. A woman with a dog could be an image of Fidelity—but in this picture the roles are reversed (and so by the same token is the role of the painter, who was ordinarily more interested in sin as a human expression than in virtue).

In any event Brouwer is known to have dealt with the Deadly Sins, for Lucas Vorsterman engraved a series of seven prints after Brouwer's designs.[1] Of four of these the original paintings seem to have been preserved; all are ovals, while the prints are rectangular.

Ira and *Pigritia* seem to belong together. The former (Bode 75; at one time in the hands of 98 the dealer Duveen in New York; a second example was formerly in the M. Kann Collection; 15.5 × 12.5 cm.) depicts an irate cavalier in a plumed hat drawing his sword. In the latter (Bode 73; 15.5 × 12.5 cm.; restored to Paris in 1954 from Munich) a lazy woman sits, inclined toward the left, her elbow resting on the table. Along with these two, although somewhat larger, is *Superbia* in the museum in Berlin-Dahlem (Bode 74; 18 × 13.5 cm.). An elegantly dressed, worldly old woman is pinning a brooch to her collar, seated before a dressing table with mirror.

Gula is represented by a greedy young peasant wearing a tall hat with a pipe stuck in it. Seated behind a table on which are a piece of paper with tobacco on it and some fragments of a pipe, he holds a large jug in both hands, and with a grin presses it to his heart (in the Liechtenstein Collection; Bode 76; 19 × 14 cm.).

There are no painted versions known of *Invidia* or of *Luxuria*, a theme that one does not expect Brouwer to handle. There was a small painted version of the *Avaritia* in the Czernin 99 Collection in Vienna: a man in a red hat hugging a money-bag. Judging from the reproduction,

[1] H. Hijmans, 'Lucas Vorsterman'; Bruxelles, 1893, Nos. 117-123.

98. PIGRITIA
Formerly Bayerische Staatsgemäldesammlungen, Munich

99. AVARITIA
Coll. Czernin, Vienna

100. MAN WITH BREAD AND SAUSAGE
Coll. Liechtenstein, Vaduz

148

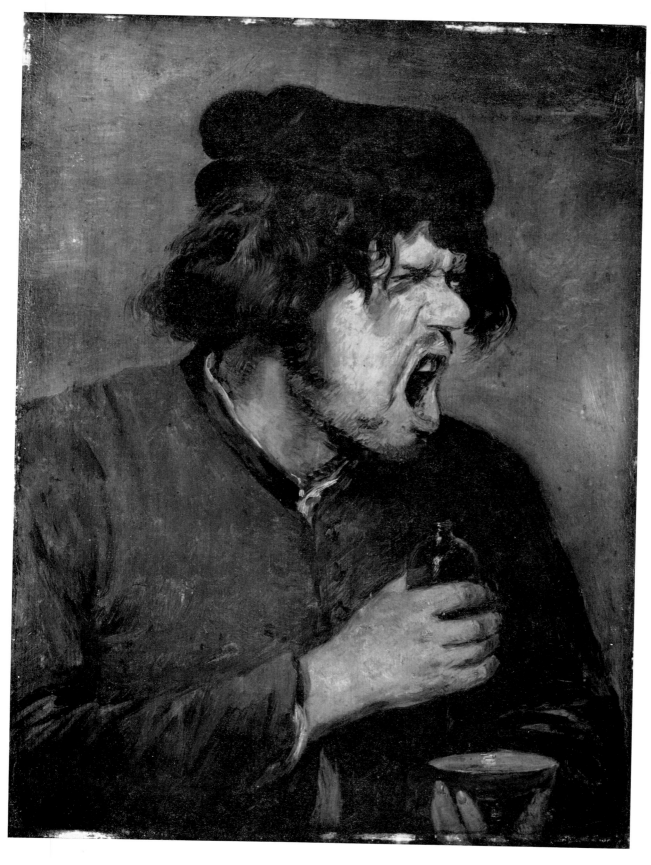

101. BITTER MEDICINE

Staedelsches Kunstinstitut, Frankfort a.M.

149

this does not seem to be an original. In the engraved series Luxuria is shown by a sumptuously drawn nude, sitting on a bed.

Nor is the original model for *Taste*, Vorsterman's eighth print after Brouwer, known.[1]

Ira, Pigritia and Superbia (although the last is on a smaller scale) presumably stem from the period of the Tobacco Inn in the Louvre, whereas the smoother, more freely painted Gula makes an other impression.

100   Perhaps related is a scene also in the Liechtenstein Collection in Vaduz: a *Man with Bread and Sausage* and a badly tousled head of hair, slily and greedily laughing, with his right hand takes a delicious titbit from the board before him, on which are lying half-eaten pieces of bread and sausage (19×14 cm.; like Avaritia, an oval).

The well-known painting in Frankfort of the man with a wry face, wide-open mouth and a
101   bottle in one hand (Bode 119; 47.5×35.5 cm.), the so-called *Bitter Medicine*, belongs to a class by itself, particularly because it is the only picture on an almost lifelike scale. It may represent Taste. Sketchily painted, it is entirely in brown, with purplish touches in the cap and greenish tints in the jacket.

Would the painting reproduced in Bode of a *Man With a Skull* who looks like a Rhetorician (Bode 122; formerly in the hands of the art-dealer Goudstikker; 19.7×16 cm.) be by Brouwer? He wears a beret and long hair, a sort of cloak is thrown over his shoulders like a drapery; while he sings or recites he holds the skull before him, and a pipe in his left hand: evidences that a Vanitas-scene is intended. It is by now clear that Bode's authority is not conclusive, however positively he may give his opinions. The reproduction does not rule out Brouwer's authorship—but gives it little support.

102   Is the stubble-bearded *Head of a Peasant* gazing upwards to the right, with his right hand on his breast, an original Brouwer? (In the Heldring Collection, Oosterbeek, Holland; Bode 80; 23.5×19 cm.). The technique, somewhat gruff yet moist and playful, does not entirely accord with any other work. Nor is there any other instance in Brouwer's œuvre of such a work as this, with no attribute or attendant circumstance offered to explain the

---

([1]) Hijmans, *op. cit.*, No. 125. The only print which is not a mirror-image of the painted version is Ira. This may be explained by the fact that if the image of the infuriated man had been reversed, he would have had to be drawing the sword from his right hip with his left hand, while in the other pictures left and right would make no difference. There are still other small differences. The facial expressions in the prints are almost consistently more pronounced—more obviously related to the meaning. Brouwer did not see human expressions in such an uncomplicated fashion. The paper with the tobacco and the pipe on it has been omitted from the print of Gula: apparently Vorsterman found the jug sufficient to express the idea. He may also have elaborated this jug: he changed it from earthenware to pewter and added a handsome lid. But why did the haughty old woman in Superbia receive a carnation, beautifully embroidered on her collar—out of place, in fact, on these ruffles. A Luxuria, a sumptuous and beautifully painted nude may even exist somewhere, unrecognized as Brouwer's because it is so completely outside the framework of his œuvre.

102. UNIDENTIFIED PAINTER, HEAD OF A PEASANT
Coll. J. C. H. Heldring, Oosterbeek (Holland)

searching upward look—although there are of course other instances of emphatic character or expression-study. The complicated, life-like expression cannot be described by any one term, such as Hofstede de Groot's 'Kopf eines wütenden Bauern'.

This picture would seem to be connected with several curious scenes of single figures making strange grimaces. These figures have explanatory attributes, which again seem to point to parabolic significance. In one is an extraordinarily *Savage Type in a Fur Cap*, with a pipe clenched

151

103. YOUTH (ACTUAL SIZE)
Coll. W. Reineke, Amersfoort (Holland)

in his right fist and a jug in the left. The idiotic grin is indeed worthy of Brouwer—or is it perhaps a bit too simplistic? (Museum in Amiens; Bode 82; 16 × 13 cm.).

A *Man With a Great Cocked Hat* has his right arm on a tall jug, and reaches his other arm out to the right of the picture. This composition is known in more than one copy, among others that in the auction in Berlin on the 10th of March, 1937, No. 57. (Less good is Bode 81, formerly in the collection of M. van Gelder in Ukkel, Belgium).

103   A *Youth Wearing a Tall Fur Cap* with a knife stuck in it: he makes a face by pulling apart the corners of his mouth with his index fingers. In front of him is a board with a jug and a glass. A repulsive but clever and acute facial study, and a skilfully executed example of Brouwer's later period. (Collection W. Reineke, Amersfoort, Holland.)

Still more terrifying is a *Fantastic Man's Head* in Dresden; he wears a cap, and the little finger of his left hand is in his mouth. Really a miniature (Bode 63; 11.5 × 8.5 cm.), it is a very strong painting which makes a blood-red impression (the jacket is purple-red; the cap

152

104. MAN WITH A POINTED HAT (ACTUAL SIZE)
Museum Boymans-van Beuningen, Rotterdam

brown). The background is of brown wooden planking. It is beautifully painted with thin, moist colours. If this picture represents Insanity, it demonstrates once again Brouwer's ability to identify himself with such tragic mental states. Another grimace: the unkempt head, covered with a beret, of a *Young Man With Only a Couple of Teeth*, bent over more from pain than mirth (formerly with the art-dealer Duits, London; 11.5 × 9.5 cm.); it has the look of a solid, sharp, cleverly painted picture.

More cheerful than the preceding is the picture of a somewhat *Tipsy Man* who looks toward the beholder over his right arm: he winks one eye; the hair under his beret is disordered; on

153

the right is his glass (S. A. Morrison Collection, London). Perhaps it is a little too tidily painted for Brouwer; might it be by Teniers?

A miniature of 8 cm. diameter (formerly in the Schloss Collection; Bode 64, left; 8 × 8 cm.): a *Young Man With a Bulbous Nose* looks with one eye closed over his right shoulder; again a beret sits on top of a wild mop of hair. It is apparently very thinly and sensitively painted; the tiny roguish, laughing, leering right eye and the mocking, half-open mouth are priceless. One would like to regard it as an early Antwerp work, like the unrelated painting with which it was framed when in the Schloss Collection. This second miniature, a *Laughing Young Man With a Beret and a Glass*, has the character of a portrait; it is a very fine, witty, attractive work (Bode 64, right; 8 × 6 cm.).

104   The same holds true for the profile of a *Man With a Pointed Hat* in the Museum Boymans-van Beuningen in Rotterdam (Bode 121; 17 × 12 cm.); he has a moustache and a pointed beard. His huge, high, pointed hat has an upturned brim: a grand little picture. The attribution to Brouwer seems to be entirely acceptable; still one wonders whence this certitude when there are so few established works having any connection with such a portrait. On the other hand, it is surely in Brouwer's spirit; and who else would have painted such a fine, amusing, penetrating, yet pictorially treated little masterwork?[1]

The attribution of another small panel (18 × 10 cm.) to Brouwer is more questionable. It shows another man in a similar hat, but now turned to the right, and might well be a counterpart to the other. It makes, however, an entirely different impression: the light background, the more pointed expression, the more cursory technique with all sorts of crosshatchings bring Teniers to mind.

5. OUTDOOR SCENES FROM THE ANTWERP PERIOD

Brouwer painted country scenes in Antwerp also, but perhaps not until some time after his arrival; at least the Antwerp landscapes are not clearly related to those compositions with many rather small figures, such as the Peasants Dancing, which may have originated either in the late Dutch or the early Antwerp years. For the remaining outside scenes display an essentially different character that marks them as belonging to the later years. One must distinguish

(1) What Bode had in mind when he wrote of this painting: 'ein Profilbild von "Jan de Dood", der populären Gestalt des Renommisten aus Brederos Lustspielen,' (p. 175) escapes me. This Boaster (Renommist) is not only not popular, but he is not to be found in Bredero's work either. Moreover, what is the evidence for this identification? Doubt has been expressed above about the absolute certainty of ascribing this work to Brouwer. We must remember that there is room for doubt regarding most of the works taken up here. The standard is really whether one could think of such a figure, executed just in this way, as a detail from a known, authentic composition. The danger with these ascriptions is that they rest on comparisons among the works themselves. Which work is to serve as the reliable starting point?

105. TOOTH PULLER (ACTUAL SIZE)
Coll. Liechtenstein, Vaduz

155

between the figure pieces, in which the landscape is no more than background, and landscapes in which the figures appear as no more than props.

The first group is related to works already considered. A typical example is the so-called *Louse Cracker* (Bode 120; New York Historical Society): many copies are known, but none recommends itself as the original. In the worst versions, the landscape is entirely missing; sometimes the man is occupied with skinning an eel, and in one case he is holding a large jug in his hands. In all probability there was an original Brouwer behind these pictures, and it must have been an interesting one: the man is working in front of a small flame, which lights up both his hands and his ruffian face, beneath the soft hat with turned-down brim. Behind is a distant landscape with typical Brouwer tree-tops, romantically lit by the moon. Another surprise in Brouwer's curiously compounded emotional life. After all the foregoing, there can be no doubt that this man, who was always compelled to witness to the degraded wretchedness of people who were victims of narcotic smoking, alcohol, gambling, and who liked to add a swine for the sake of comparison, hankered after peace and quiet, after tenderness and tranquillity. It is striking how often he would leave the top half of the door of a stuffy inn open, to clear a way, as it were, into the free outdoor atmosphere; and in a few cases he gives something more than a solitary abridged indication of the atmosphere. His actual country scenes are not only rest—recreative interruption from a life of altogether differently directed work—but are an essential element of his life and an escape from it. They embody the ultimate attainment of freedom. Perhaps the way to it was first fully cleared for him through the contacts and inspirations of his last years (Rubens, Lievens). In any case we intend here (on grounds, in the first place, of intuition) to place these paintings later in his development, according to the degree in which the free landscape forms a more essential element in them.

Surely intuition is warranted, since nothing is known with objective certainty. Even in a very short life, the works produced after the first thirty years will be those manifesting greatest equilibrium and a wise contemplative spirit—at least if the evolution develops organically. Works of an entirely different spirit may come into being at this time, and unless the development is somehow disturbed, these balanced works will not be produced at any earlier stage. One must, in Brouwer's case, consider the possibility of such a disturbance; for, although the evidence for it is not very convincing, tradition speaks of it repeatedly. The Smokers in New York, however, demonstrates that Brouwer, at a time not much more than one year before the end of his activity, was in complete possession of his powers; and this painting also has elements which point in the direction of his landscape art.

There is still other support for our intuition. In Brouwer's œuvre there are really only two paintings which can claim to be considered portraits: the selfportrait in the Mauritshuis and the man with a dog in the Heldring Collection (the Good Comrades). Both have something of a

106. BALL PLAYERS
Musées Royaux des Beaux Arts, Brussels

157

landscape quality about them; and this landscape is of a most discreet, refined, intimate type, as if the quiet and simple study of man in his every-day appearance went hand in hand with the peaceful atmosphere of this background. Accordingly they are connected with the very simple landscape in the Academy in Vienna, where everything is excluded that might disturb the unity of the atmosphere. This Vienna scene can only represent the final stage, or at least one aspect of it. A notable painting in the Liechtenstein Gallery in Vaduz seems to confirm this conception of Brouwer's development. An *Itinerant Tooth Puller* (Bode 25; 23 × 17 cm.) draws a tooth from a patient's mouth, while his wife stands by to assist. A familiar Brouwer theme, but somewhat changed in conception. The three people have come closer together. The surgeon is distinguished not only by his close attention to his task, but a new element, concern for his patient, has been introduced; and on the patient's part we observe an element of yielding, of trust in the physician. The woman is strangely attired and is depicted almost as a caricature. Yet she too manifests something of willingness to serve, and of solicitude. This scene is unusually light in tone; the action takes place in the inner courtyard of a castle, perhaps one of those typical Brabant castle farms. The outside atmosphere has been expressed in entirely new tone-relationships. There is space and a blond light in the air. How different and how much further developed this is than in the landscapes from the late Dutch period; one can well believe that a number of years has intervened between the two periods of landscape activity.

The scene is set, now in a wide space under a grand, open sky—but in an enclosed courtyard. This also may be taken as a definite compositional element, limited by certain psychic inhibitions. As such it recurs in the fine Brussels painting the *Ball Players* (Bode 84; 22.5 × 21 cm.).

Outside an inn, which one does not see, is a long, rude table with benches on either side. It is on the left-hand side of the scene, standing in a sandy lot which is separated by a long fence of battered upright boards from a small, rounded dune, almost bare of vegetation. Into this fence is built a privy; the door stands open and inside sits the familiar, grotesque little man, while another is urinating nearby. On the right a hog. On the left four men sit at the table and a fifth stands next to it: typical Brouwer people with pipe and jug. But the mood is one of pleasant talk, during an interlude in a game played with balls which have to be aimed through a small iron ring. The man sitting with his back to the beholder, in a yellow jacket and large, light-grey hat, looks to be an outsider in this group. There is little other colour, except for the strong blue of the sky, with its white clouds. The roof on the right showing above the fence provides a fine red note. Brouwer has, out of these anomalous elements, constructed a wonderfully precious idyll, with limited data and colour, in a full but fluent touch—in tune with the small format. Everything here is very sensitively 'in tune': note, for example, the very carefully and tellingly painted iron ring and the two wooden balls on the bare, blond

XII. Selfportrait
Mauritshuis, The Hague

sand. It is a very great master who can make a complete, vivid still life out of an iron ring and two small balls on a stretch of sand. How exquisite is the dune behind the fence with two small figures near the top: nothing distinguishes it except the undulations of the ground and the extremely meager vegetation; the fine silver-grey and faint pallid tone of the atmosphere about it has been represented with exquisite subtlety.

What a strange man! Does this painting not represent an attempt to escape from the realm of passion, corruption and sordidness which he came back to again and again—yet with precisely the same men and still in a markedly limited space?[1]

A more softened Brouwer appears with ever-increasing clarity at the end of his short life. There is a small panel in the Heldring Collection, of a man with his dog (Bode 101; 16 × 13 cm.), painted in a bluish tone except for the russet of the hat. Not unjustly it has received the rather sentimental-sounding title the *Good Comrades*. This is, in fact, the content of the scene; nor is it pure fantasy, but rather a portrait of some definite man with his friend. How intensely has this friendship been imagined. And again it is set out-of-doors: dunish country, sketched in the new thin airiness, under a very fine sky. And again nothing about this coarse vagrant— or is he a game-keeper?—is idealized. 107 108

Finally there is the famous *Portrait of a Man* (Bode 6; 24 × 16 cm.; Mauritshuis, The Hague). XII The notion that this is a self-portrait has later been rejected. It would not agree with the portraits of Brouwer by Lievens and van Dyck or with The Smokers in New York. But the recent find of a portrait of Brouwer by van Craesbeeck makes it plausible that this painting in the Mauritshuis may yet be a self-portrait of Brouwer.[2] The colours are limited to brown and, in the background, tender shades of green and yellow before the dune-like landscape and the dark sky. The manner of painting is extremely sensitive and thin, executed with a short brushstroke. The rugged head, with the wild hair, moustache, and unkempt little beard are carefully and surely built up with many tone shadows. Note the scintillating way in which the light effects have been applied to the collar and shirt, along his forehead and cheek, and in his eye. In the landscape, apparently so casual and sketchily done, Brouwer has concealed a few sensitive details, such as the walking couple and the bird in the sky.

Brouwer could have become a great portrait painter, but of a very personal, genre-like type of portrait, related to Frans Hals more than to anyone else.

Can such a painter have executed the genuine portrait piece the *Four Children* in the von

---

([1]) Bode regarded this as the painter's earliest landscape; I think I have shown good reason for regarding it as one of his last—unless all were painted at the very end of his career. This does away with the old tradition that the scene is a memento of Brouwer's sojourn in the Citadel at Antwerp. A dune, not a bastion, rises behind the fence, and the latter would make a poor wall for a castle used as a prison.

([2]) See further Appendix E, p. 181.

107. GOOD COMRADES (ACTUAL SIZE)
Coll. J. C. H. Heldring, Oosterbeek (Holland)

Pannwitz Collection (Bode 89; 35 × 50 cm.) ascribed to him? Its tone is entirely different from that of his other works.[1]

It was, of course, a commission; which fact alone is an adequate explanation of the divergent character of this small work. Moreover, the artist who painted the Good Comrades in the Heldring Collection can be entrusted with the sensitive depiction of these four well-bred, elegantly dressed small children. Above all, the beautiful, very romantic landscape with the

[1] Judging only from reproductions I was inclined to reject this exceptional work; but Frits Lugt, who knows the original well, pleaded Brouwer's authorship with such assurance, that I thought fit not to set aside the judgement of such an eminent authority.

108. GOOD COMRADES (DETAIL)

161

109. TWILIGHT
Musée du Louvre, Paris

group of trees handled in a characteristically Brouwer fashion is entirely in his spirit, as is the piquant contrast between this background and the portrait group—so unlike the charming landscape idyll that an other artist would have thought suited to this motif. The bird on the stick held by the standing child is a Brouwer touch. Such small inventions are very much in Brouwer's spirit and are here executed in his subtle way.

The romantic element of this background reappears in Brouwer's pure landscapes. These are, in the later years as in the earlier, far from exclusively idyllic. The master, who apparently often fled from the stifling confinement of Antwerp, knew well the opposite side of the medal.

109   There is in the Louvre the ominous and breathtaking landscape of *Twilight* (Bode 98; 17 × 26 cm.). Brouwer's interest here was not in contrasting effects. A strong wind is sweeping through the tops of the scrubby dune trees, broadly and forcefully painted. Half hidden is a grey house, with no welcoming entrance visible. It is probably an inn, since there are several recent customers outside in a dishevelled condition. In the foreground a man totters unsteadily, leaning on his cane, and on the right another man squats down to relieve himself. A third is making water against a wall. Two couples are coming from the house, but by no

162

110. Road near a House (actual size)

Courtesy of the John G. Johnson Collection, Philadelphia

163

III. LANDSCAPE WITH FULL MOON
Staatliche Museen, Berlin-Dahlem

means in loving embrace: it looks as if one woman is about to be murdered, and the shadowy pair further back does not seem to be on any better terms. Did these women come to fetch their drunken men from the inn?

The painting is broad, forceful, gruff and dynamic; the colour of the trees is almost black. The sky on the left is blue but, above is a heavy, dark, brown streak. In the vegetation on the sandy ground at the right there are many touches of colour.

Between the two extremes of this ominous twilight and the idyllic mood of, for example, the Ball Players in Brussels, falls Brouwer's late landscape. No sequence appears clearly in these pictures. Taken together with the last interior scenes, such as the small picture of two fighting men in Munich, they demonstrate the vacillations in the artist's emotional life. Relaxation of tension is by no means always evident in the works of the last years, but it was coming increasingly to the fore at the end. He painted a few pure landscapes at this time, in which this escape manifests itself more clearly.

164

112. BALL PLAYERS
Staatliche Museen, Berlin-Dahlem

In the Johnson Collection in Philadelphia hangs a *Road near a House* (Bode 99; 24.1 × 18.1 cm.) 110
with a road leading to a house on the left behind a hummock of sand, and on the right a pole
with a signboard and a posted notice. A narrow path runs between the low dunes. Something
is wrong with this path: it is too narrow, as in a lilliput landscape; or is the scale of the figures
too large? The background is wooded. The treatment puts one in mind of the small painting in
Paris, but lacks the impetus of the latter. The figures look like Brouwer's at first sight, but are
clumsy and misshapen. They are five in all: a couple disappearing into the background; a
very short, badly proportioned fellow with a pack under his arm and a stick, and two arguing
men in the foreground, not much more successful than the last. A Brouwer? The objections
mentioned argue against it, still... it is a very beautiful little painting, with a luminous
cobalt-blue above the horizon. The mood is penetrating. The figure in the middle is a dull
terra-cotta, the dune is brown and greenish; above is a splendid wild sky.

Regarding another landscape also I cannot make out whether the original is better than
the reproduction would suggest; a small *Landscape*, with five men in the foreground playing at
ninepins, at one time with the art-dealer Paul Graupe in New York (26.8 × 35.8 cm.). This too is

165

certainly of the Brouwer-type and is very close to the Johnson Collection landscape, but the technique is different (as in the tall tree on the right); a strange note is the pile of sand heaped up by the wind; and the men are somewhat clumsier.

This same sort of squat figure appears again, in the *Landscape* with an extensive view and three men talking in the foreground (Patridge Collection, London; Bode 86; 28 × 34.9 cm.); but in this case the landscape departs from Brouwer's style. How could the master of the vista behind the Four Children in the von Pannwitz Collection have painted this one? Those queer little men seem to have become a reason for ascribing a picture to Brouwer!

The case is quite different with a very pretty and carefully elaborated landscape showing a *Shepherd Boy Playing the Flute*; the picture is of an unexpectedly large size (Bode 91; 49 × 84 cm.; Berlin-Dahlem Museum). Considerable overpainting is clearly visible, in some places covering up partly men and animals (sheep, among others). These overpaintings make moreover a mouldy impression. But even disregarding them, there does not seem to be anything of Brouwer here. All is too tame and sweet and well-finished. Compare it with the landscape in the Academy in Vienna that will be discussed shortly. To attribute to Brouwer an Arcadian idyll with a shepherd boy playing the flute, his faithful dog near him, is really going too far!

Nor are there any better grounds for ascribing an other *Landscape with a Resting Traveller* in the same museum to him. In the foreground the traveller, seen from the rear, sits (Bode 93; 40 × 35 cm.); how poorly painted is his back, and even more so his oversized seat. On the left lies his travelling gear, basket and jug: the touch of the sensitive still-life painter is as absent here as is that of the great landscapist in the surrounding scenery.

There are, however, two other small landscapes in Berlin-Dahlem where one finds Brouwer in his best form.

111 First, the *Landscape Under a Full Moon* shining on a broad expanse of water (probably the Hont or Westerschelde) is an intensely moodful scene (Bode 90; 25 × 34 cm.). On the right is a cottage straight from a fairy-tale. On the left three men stand talking: functioning merely as objects in space, they are only blocked in; still they do not belong with the clumsy type described above. A couple on the shore appears to be admiring the moonlight effect on the water. In the left middleground a tower, beyond are sailboats: all in all a dream-world, ethereal in the light of the moon, which is painted in front of a pitch-black gap in the clouds. There is hardly any colour: the rest of the water and the sky is grey; there is a vague touch of terra-cotta in the foreground.

112 Second, the *Ball Players* (Bode 88; 23.5 × 33.5 cm.): as in the Brussels Ball Players, the ball is to be driven through the ring. The farm buildings, elaborately painted, probably are used as an inn as well, to judge from the number of men standing about and from the fact that there is a special place for playing the game. The house type is that of the Kempen region,

XIII. Dune Landscape

Akademie der Bildenden Künste, Vienna

where Vincent van Gogh rediscovered it later.[1] The rather scraggy trees go with this sort of country. On the left is a distant view with a bulky tower. Above, a wild, romantic sky, with grazing touches of light. The picture is freely and spontaneously painted in a constantly changing, sometimes impasto manner. The figures are like those in the Moonlight Landscape: not extensively worked out, they are conceived only as props. There is something exceptionally spontaneous about this little painting.

Finally we come to the *Dune Landscape* in the Akademie of Vienna (Bode 95; 26 × 36 cm.). XIII It is as if the background of the portrait in the Mauritshuis or that in the Good Comrades had been worked up into an independent picture. The elements here are as few and are as vaguely and indecisively represented; thereby they dissolve as lightly into space and relate themselves to it naturally. Here, indeed, space is the subject: on the right the vault of the lofty sky rises above a low horizon. Under these arching heavens, in front of which glides a heavy cloud, Brouwer has realized the forms of phenomena hesitantly, reflectively. A man stands talking quietly with a youth seated on the ground; there are some touches of russet, dark violet and blue-grey here· As in the Selfportrait in the Mauritshuis and in the Brussels Ball Players, there is another figure standing on the dune.

The colour is thin, very fair, on the right almost ivory, with some brown and greyish greens. The green lies like foam on the top of the low dune at the left. In the distance there is some slate-blue, but the sky is, above all, light. The heavier black-brown of the left foreground has been brushed in as if caught in a gust of wind. The manner of painting has such musical touches everywhere.

Could this be Brouwer's last work? We would like to think so. It would be a suitable end to his ever more enigmatic life. For many years he tried to smother his need for tenderness and intimacy in the stark representation of sordidness, coarseness, and wretchedness—in the end to find release through this sublime rarification.

6. THE DRAWINGS

The drawings raise the same problem as the paintings, in that there are few that can be ascribed to Brouwer with certainty, but many more claiming his name. There is no conclusively proved Brouwer drawing, so that the latitude for ascriptions becomes accordingly broader. No sheet documented as an original by his signature or in any other way is known. In the biographical tales the drawings figure as a currency used on the spot to pay for food and drink. It is safe to assume that Brouwer made sketches from nature. But we can only guess what

(¹) See the note n. 2, p. 19.

167

they looked like—keeping in mind that his great artistry would have left its imprint on them.

In almost every great print cabinet one encounters drawings under his name. These attributions are based on the nature of the representations, showing analogy with Brouwer paintings, and on the name given to them, often in the eighteenth or nineteenth century (and almost always corrupted to such a form as BRAUER, BRAWER, BRAUR or the like). Not without reasons do the museums keep to such unconvincing attributions, often against their better judgment, in filing away these drawings: only in this way can they keep track of them amidst their vast material; and they generally have some connection with Brouwer's art.

The number which has been ascribed to Brouwer on sufficient grounds seems to be 113 very small indeed. There is a group of sketch pages (in the print cabinets in Berlin, Hamburg, 114 Dresden and the Victoria and Albert Museum, London) ($\pm$ 22 × 33 cm.) on which are 115 scattered typical Brouwer figures and groups, reminiscent of similar sheets by Bosch. The pen-strokes are rapid and dashing, spirited and yet exactly right, succinct, and tense; on some the shadow is put in with a smooth bister wash. They are masterful sketches, which fully answer to the genius of the young artist. The crux of the matter is the limited, remarkably 'stenographic' means of expression in the summary pen-strokes, and their extraordinarily dynamic expressive power. A single figure, or a pair together is sketched either in some moment of physical tension, or in intense concentration on a task. Remarkably seldom are the motifs related to those met with in Brouwer's paintings, which points to their origin as momentary images of what caught Brouwer's eye, or of what effervesced from his spirit.

The style of drawing is diametrically opposed to the carefulness with which Brouwer executed his paintings: it may be regarded as the complement of this carefulness: it is quick, condensed, synthesized; intended either simply as 'five-finger exercises', or to capture the essence of an idea or happening—or perhaps, as was Rembrandt's practice—to collect material regarding stances, gestures and bearings for use in his paintings. But all indication of surroundings, of scenery is wanting. They are no more than sketches, the same figure or group often being repeated several times, scattered disconnectedly on the paper, yet with the instinctive, infallible feeling for composition which makes such a sheet a work of art. The unerring directness which was retained in the painted compositions appears here at its sharpest. There is an analogy between this relationship and that of Rembrandt's first sketches and his finished works. One should not forget, however, that this attribution to Brouwer—tempting though it may be—is only a hypothesis, based on the emotional conviction that Brouwer would have drawn like this. Also the clothes as well as the figures in the drawings are somewhat more old-fashioned than in the paintings, and they are devoted to portraying a typical peasant humour, more in the spirit of Bosch and of Pieter Bruegel the Elder than that revealed in Brouwer's paintings: for example a woman thrashing her husband, and more or

113. PAGE FROM A SKETCHBOOK
Victoria and Albert Museum, London

114. PAGE FROM A SKETCHBOOK
Hamburger Kunsthalle

169

less scurrilous jokes. Yet . . . the attribution to Brouwer is so attractive. The dynamic element, the expression of action is entirely in his line rather than that of the sixteenth-century masters just mentioned. Their work and style has been continued here—emphatically so—but with a concern for movement and precedence of movement over matter unknown in the sixteenth century. It is as if in these sketches one had come upon the figures found in Brouwer's paintings in their basic form, in their essential character as sources of energy. They are probably early works by Brouwer, from the period when he was a learner and was collecting material for study. They may date from about the time of his moving from Holland to Antwerp. They are doubtless not the drawings which he is said to have sketched in Antwerp taverns and offered as payment for his bills. They are not scenes such as he would have observed there. Their humour is more in line with the chaff and wry banter of the Haarlem and Amsterdam periods than with the more dynamic Antwerp work. As is evident from the somewhat older work of Goltzius, with his imitations of Dürer and Lucas van Leyden, there was considerable interest in Haarlem in the sixteenth-century masters; at any rate these drawings are inconceivable without the example of Bosch and of Pieter Bruegel—the latter highly regarded by Haarlem painters.

These sheets, to judge from the similarity of paper and of size, appear to have come originally from a single sketchbook, and to have originated, therefore, at about the same time. A 117 leaf in Besançon of a somewhat smaller format (15 × 21 cm.) with sketches on both sides, is 118 closely related to them. The figures fill the pages a bit more, they are slightly more solid and are more amply modelled. One motif, known from a painting, appears here: the father's disagreeable task. The painting of this subject we assigned to the beginning of the Antwerp years. Accordingly the place in the œuvre for these sheets would come somewhat later than the large sketch-book leaves, which dating would accord well with the impression that they make.

In the Van Regteren Altena Collection in Amsterdam is a sheet which has many points of agreement with the first group of drawings. The style is less certain and less accurate. A few heavier lines, such as those along the under side of some thighs and the lower legs, move rather more calligraphically than dynamically. It is difficult to decide whether these sketches are by an other hand than Brouwer's. They are apparently studies for an Adoration of the Shepherds, which does not argue for a Brouwer attribution.

In the Carton de Tournai Collection in Brussels is a sketch of a tavern interior which 116 departs still further from the type discussed. It is a lively and spontaneous drawing, not without merits, but more likely a clever jotting made after a composition by Brouwer than a direct original work by him. For they contain too much that does not contribute to the clear expression of form or of an element of form.

115. PAGE FROM A SKETCHBOOK
Staatliche Museen, Berlin-Dahlem

117. PAGE FROM A SKETCHBOOK
Musée des Beaux-Arts, Besançon

Two sketches are listed under Brouwer's name in Bayonne. In one a woman is cooking, while behind are a handful of tavern customers at a table and a sort of choir of three monk-like figures and a standing hurdy-gurdy player. The second sketch is so dissimilar that it surely cannot be by the same hand; in any case it is not by Brouwer. The first would be more at home in the school of Rembrandt; I find no connection between Brouwer's art and such a subject as singing monks.

Many other similar drawings, often closer to the style of Ostade, need not be gone into here.

The six large sketch-book pages and the two smaller ones in Besançon probably all represent a quite short period in Brouwer's development and do not in themselves rule out another sort of drawing: to wit, a series from a small sketch-book in the print cabinet in Stockholm. These are, however, entirely dissimilar in manner, their lines being crude, insensitively scratched in, and slap-dash; and they lack the tension and directness of the above sketches; their quality is so far inferior that one can only explain the attribution to Brouwer by recourse to the fact that they are all marked 'Adrien Braur'. (Four were reproduced by Bode as late works.)

Other drawings ascribed to Brouwer are seldom comparable to those first discussed in spirit or in masterly accuracy.

A drawing, *Woman Spanking her Child*, in the Albertina in Vienna (Bode 47) has a motif which is comparable to the Father's Disagreeable Task in Dresden, and at first glance it is full of tension and lively action; but it displays weaknesses and misdrawing (the raised arm, the knees of the man on the left, the figure of the man looking round the door) which render belief in it as a Brouwer autograph difficult.

The sketch related to the large tavern scene in the National Gallery (Bacon Collection), 69 also in the Albertina (Bode 109, where it is incorrectly supposed to be in Dresden), was discussed when we considered this painting (p. 114).

Other instances of sketches related to known paintings are clearly inferior imitations of entire compositions or of a few figures. Brouwer's figures, strongly characterized, often tending toward caricature and always witty, lent themselves to copying or imitation; and former generations did not have our scruples against adding the ostensible signature of the master to such imitations. But a critical examination, proceeding from the assumption that a master such as Brouwer can never completely belie his great artistry, can distinguish without difficulty most of these imitations.

For only one drawing must an exception be made, because it shows so many analogies with what is typical in Brouwer's painted œuvre, and moreover because it has the high quality to 119 justify regarding it as an original. The *Head of a Young Man* in the Heldring Collection is sketched in a free, broad and telling manner: its verve, accuracy, and immediacy preclude any de-

118. PAGE FROM A SKETCHBOOK
Musée des Beaux-Arts, Besançon

116. PAGE WITH SKETCHES, ASCRIBED TO BROUWER
Coll. Baron Carton de Tournai, Brussels

173

pendence on a prior work of art; and finally the artist's epigrammatic vision of the boy points conclusively to the master's hand. By means of this drawing we can imagine how the older, more mature Brouwer must have sketched his models.

119. HEAD OF A YOUNG MAN
Coll. J. C. H. Heldring, Oosterbeek (Holland)

APPENDICES

APPENDIX A

(TO PP. 30—32 PL. 2—5)

WORKS BY THE PAINTER OF THE LARGE JARS

Below is a list of works by the 'Painter of the Large Jars', assembled from the reproductions in the Rijks-bureau voor Kunsthistorische Documentatie in The Hague. Facts concerning location and size also come from the Rijksbureau. The paintings are listed in what I consider most likely to be the chronological order. I append critical observations and conclusions.

1. *Singing Trio behind a Table*, (half-figures) on which table are a large jar, a table-stove and tobacco. The singer on the left has a pipe in his mouth; he wears a sort of cowl with a long lappet hanging over his shoulder—a characteristic detail for this painter. Warneck Auction, Paris, 27 May, 1926.

2. 2. *Peasants Carousing* (half-figures); the table made out of a plank on top of a barrel. The left-hand figure holds up a rummer; the man on the right wears the same kind of head-dress as the man on the left of No. 1, above. On the table is a jar, a table-stove, and a pipe; there is another jar on a tabouret. City of York Art Gallery (1938 in the hands of the art-dealer H. A. Buttery, London); 22.2 × 18.1 cm.

   Sturdily and plastically, but roughly painted, as if hacked out of wood with bold strokes, a technique completely contrary to Brouwer's. But the motif, like that of the foregoing painting, *may* have been painted by Brouwer.

3. 3. *Three Singers in a Room* (half-figures); the door in the background is open and three men are coming in. The singer on the right, seen frontally, sits behind a desk on which rests an open book. Next to him is a fiddler, on whose left is a singer with the typical cowl, and raised hand. In the foreground on a sort of chest are a thick book, a jar and a glass bottle. On the wall there hang a painting and a cup. Amsterdam, Rijksmuseum; panel; 39 × 26 cm.

   Similarly broad, but somewhat more loosely painted than No. 2. The same types, the same sort of humour.

4. *Foolish Gods*. Among the clouds are four heads caricaturing the antique gods: in front, Neptune; on the right, Mars; on the left, Mercury and Apollo. Neptune has the same head as the man behind the desk in No. 3; Mars as that of the first man entering. Buchenau Collection, Neindorf, Germany; panel; 16 × 13.8 cm.

   The style departs markedly from the foregoing: neither hard nor wooden, it is rather fluent and woolly. But the two heads mentioned are so clearly the same as those in the previous painting that there must be a close connection between the two. The broad character also persists. Did the differ nature of the representation elicit a different style? Or was there another hand working with large-jar master?

5. *Mussel-Eaters*. An interior with five full-length figures of the type already observed, rende

176

the rough, angular manner. There are three jugs in the right foreground. Private Collection, London; panel; 41 × 33 cm.

Perhaps somewhat more fluently painted than Nos. 1, 2 and 3. The man with the cowl, looking up toward the woman with a plate, is rather more vivid and lively.

6. The *Smoker*, kneeling in front of the hearth, lights his pipe with a burning piece of wood. Near him 4 a monkey, a bowl of batter, three jars and a little pipe. In the background a group of five figures, painted broadly and sketchily, but with animation. In the hands of Boehler in Luzern in 1949; panel; 36.5 × 25.5 cm.

This is the most pointed and humourous painting by this artist, of a quality surpassing the foregoing. The style is more fluent and at the same time more careful, although the rough indication of the major forms remains. The characterization of the man is outstanding, as is the treatment of him. The group in the background is Brouwer-like, but conceived more as caricature. The painting fits nicely into the school of Frans Hals about 1630, in its lighter tone as in other respects.

7. *Sausage Woman*. An interior of a butcher's (a pig-carcass hangs against the wall). In the foreground is a clumsy, fat woman, who is taking a big sausage out of a deep pan over the fire. On her right are jars, a foot-stove, a platter with a sausage, a calf's head and beets. In the background there are five diners gathered around a table, a man against the wall seen from the rear, and an open door through which a man, a woman and a child exit. Art-dealer Matthiesen, Göteborg, Sweden, 1939.

The execution is characteristic, but more awkward and rougher than in the previous works; the carved-from-wood look is gradually disappearing. The group in the background is Brouwer-like in conception but is sketchily carried out in a broader, much more clumsy way. The connection with Brouwer, however, is unmistakable, while the sausage woman puts one in mind of Brouwer's pancake woman. This Large-jar painter characterizes his subjects in an almost impressionistic way.

8. *Seven Men Carousing in an Inn* (full-length). The man on the left, with cowl, has fallen asleep over 5 the back of his three-cornered chair. On the right is a smoker seen from the side, also with this headdress and with a dagger in his belt: a seedy scoundrel with a short beard and disordered hair. On the bench in the foreground are two large jars. In the doorway in the background stands a vomiting man with his wife and child. There is a little man by the fireplace. Bristol, Art Gallery; purchased in 1949 from a London art-dealer; panel, 27 × 41.2 cm.

A typical work in all respects, again using Brouwer motifs in a way characteristic of this follower.

9. *Four Smokers around a Barrel* (full-length). In the left foreground a rough figure fills his pipe; he wears a large, light, straw hat, long hair and beard, and light sleeves and breeches. Again a few large jars. J. Warner-Prins Collection, New York; panel; 25 × 22 cm.

The heads have entirely lost their carved-from-wood character; they have become rounder and more fleshy.

10. *Cutting the Stone*. The patient is in the foreground, a half-hidden figure with his knees drawn up and a contorted face. Behind him is the derisive quack. His wife looks around from behind a screen. On the left a jar in the foreground. In the hands of the art-dealer Goudstikker, Amsterdam, in 1925.

11. *Trio by the Fire*. Three men seen full-length: the one on the right plays on a jaw-bone; the one on the left, the violin. In the background a woman cleans mussels and a man leans drunkenly in, over the lower half of the door. Dresden Museum (acquired in 1928).

Broadly and fluently painted in a very clear tone. It is possibly not by this master, but has some connection with him—really too little to be a late, mature stage of his art. It is broader, freer and less sketchy; the tone and the delineation of space in the clear grey light are conspicuously finer. The figure composition is reminiscent of Brouwer, but everything has been transferred to a more comfortable sphere.

There can be little doubt that these paintings belong together and are all, except for the last, the work of a single painter. One can entertain doubts about No. 4, because it is painted in a different style (to judge from the reproductions); but the two heads are certainly repetitions of (or models for) those in No. 3. Presumably this painter is a Haarlemmer who was strongly attracted by Brouwer's example, and may even have retained some contact with Brouwer's subsequent art, after the latter had gone to Flanders. Stronger even than Brouwer's influence, which appears in the choice of motifs, in the groups in the backgrounds and in the surroundings in which the scenes are placed, is the influence of Hals and his school, especially in the vicinity of Judith Leyster and Jan Miense Molenaer. There are compositions by the latter, dating from 1630, at the beginning of his career (and shortly before Brouwer went to Antwerp) that are comparable to the above-listed works: in the sobriety of the dress, in the relationship between figures and space, in the powerful, simplified handling of the plastic delineation of form; but Molenaer's paintings are on another, more polished, delicate, skilful and aesthetically responsible level. The last-named painting in Dresden stands more or less between the two modes of expression. The 'Painter of the Large Jars' achieves a result which is individual and not unimportant, particularly in No. 6. (The man kneeling at the fire to light his pipe.) He paints—and visibly enjoys painting—an other social class, an other environment than the one Brouwer or Molenaer painted. But which one? Are these often strangely dressed people what they seem to be, or are they perhaps itinerant actors, shown relaxing in popular taverns? If the latter, they are of a lower status than the ones Schmidt-Degener correctly thought he recognized in Buytewegh's scenes. The large foreground figures in Nos. 8 and 9 particularly give the impression of being wandering actors.

APPENDIX B

WORKS BY BROUWER IN RUBENS' COLLECTION

According to van den Branden's report, Rubens' valuable art collection contained at his death 'besides the *Peasant Dance in a Landscape*, the following sixteen panels by Adriaan de Brouwer (sic): *Fighting Drunkards*, with the one pulling the other's hair; *A Tavern*, with men sitting by the fire; *A Landscape* with lightning; *Singing Peasants*; *The Jealous Peasant; A Fight* in which one man takes another by the throat; *A Landscape*; *A Landscape* with three figures, one beating another with a pot; *The Temptation of St. Anthony*; *Peasants Singing by the Fire*; *A Lute-Player*; *A Peasant* with a rummer and a pot in his hands; *Peasants Smoking*; *A Landscape* with a peasant tying his shoelaces; *Two Peasants* staring through a window; and a *Landscape* by moonlight.'

APPENDIX C

INVENTORY OF BROUWER'S POSSESSIONS IN 1632[1]

Ierst twee stucxkens in swertte lijsten, wesende Landschappen van Momper.

Item twee stucxkens swert ende wit van Sotten Cleef.

Een marmeren stucxken van Focquier.

Een contrefeytsel van sekeren persoon genoempt Theodosus.

Noch een stucxken van swert en wit, wesende eenen Keyzer sittende in sijne Majesteyt.

Een stuck, wesende eene ordinantie van eenige Sangers, gedootverft van den voorschreven Brouwer.

Noch drije andere stucxkens bij den selven gedootverft, d'een in eene swertte lijste.

Noch een pineel daerop eenen Man gedootverft staet.

Noch vijff pineeltkens, gedootverft als voore.

Eene copere plaetken daeroppe eenen Manspersoon gedootverft.

Achtthien pinceelen mette stocken.

Thien pinceelstocken.

Een houten manneken met sijn pedestael.

Drij swertte mutsen.

Eenen riem met eenen poignaert.

Een glas met verwen daerinne.

Een aergentinen cappoot met silveren galon.

Een camisoel van gevrocht swert armosijn.

Een paer swertte sattijne mouwen.

Een paer coleur sattijne mouwen.

Een swert caffa rocxken, met een broecke.

Eenen swertten laeckenen mantel, met caffa gevoedert.

Acht boecken.

Twee hoeyen.

Een caerte van de belegeringe van Breda.

Eenen omslach ende vijff poignetten.

Drij dosijnen pinceelen.

Tweelff printen.

Een spiegeltken.

([1]) Protocols of the notary Frans Marcelis, 1631-32.

APPENDIX D

LIST OF WORKS BY BROUWER IN THE ANTHONIE COLLECTION 1691

Twee cleyn Vrouwecontrefeytsels, op plaetjens, van Brouwer	gl. 72.—
Een Vrouwken met Catteken, op paneel, van Brouwer	„ 72.—
Twee Tronikens, op paneel, van Brouwer	„ 15.—
Toebackrookerken met andere Mannekens, op paneel, van Brouwer . . .	„ 350.—
Een Manneken met Roomerken in de Hand, op paneel, van Brouwer . .	„ 36.—
Een Barbierken, op paneel, van Brouwer	„ 400.—
Een Landschap, op paneel, van Brouwer	„ 12.—
Een Boerken en Boerinneken met tennen pot, op paneel, van Brouwer . .	„ 240.—
Een Landschapken met twee Mannekens, op paneel, van Brouwer . . .	„ 18.—
Een Manneken met een Sacxken, op paneel, ovael, van Brouwer . . .	„ 72.—
Een Manneken, int root, met Compagnie, aen 't Tictambert, op paneel, van Brouwer	„ 200.—
Een Maneschijntjen, op paneel, van Brouwer	„ 36.—
Een Manneken en de Vrouwken, met Conversatie van achter, op paneel, van Brouwer	„ 100.—
Eenige Mannekens aen 't Vier, op paneel, van Brouwer	„ 240.—
Een Gevecht aen een Tonne, op paneel, van Brouwer	„ 400.—
Een Boerengevecht tusschen de Deur en de Steyl, op paneel, van Brouwer . .	„ 300.—
Eenen Coninck Drinck, op paneel, van Brouwer	„ 400.—
Een Teirlinckspel, op paneel, van Brouwer	„ 150.—

APPENDIX E

A PORTRAIT OF BROUWER BY JOOS VAN CRAESBEECK
AND BROUWER'S SELF-PORTRAIT IN THE MAURITSHUIS

Since this work went to press, Dr. Walter Bernt of Munich has called my attention to a painting, marked with the Van Craesbeeck monogram, which in his opinion is a portrait of Adriaen Brouwer. I am very grateful to him for this suggestion which proves to be an interesting find. It is certainly a typical if not a particularly strong work by Van Craesbeeck, and identification of the sitter with Brouwer is convincing. In contrast to the swaggering portraits by Van Dyck and Lievens and the manner in which Brouwer portrayed himself in some of his own works (Cf. "The Smokers" in New York, also the painting in Apsley House) this picture represents the painter in a homely, unpretentious and intimate manner as if he were resting after work. Indeed, the conspicuous moustache and pointed beard are there, while the ironic smile in the eyes equally bears the stamp of the man as we imagine him to have been. Furthermore in this quite rough painting a pschycologically

JOOS VAN CRAESBEEK, PORTRAIT OF BROUWER

182

startling likeness is presented to us of this proud, critical and highly intelligent man having a moment's respite from what was for him in the natural order of things the fulfilment of his life—his exquisite creative work. We might even surmise that the dainty little handkerchief he holds in his left hand—a hand forceful even when at rest—was in fact a painter's rag, although he is hardly likely to have chosen to have himself portrayed with such an attribute!

Another consequence of Dr. Bernt's find is that this painting emphasises the probability of the famous Mauritshuis portrait being a self-portrait of Brouwer (Cf. p. 159 and No. XII). This is undoubtedly a very late work of the artist (note the subtly rarefied manner of painting and the treatment of the landscape) while the portrait by Van Craesbeeck I surmise to have been painted a couple of years later, about the year 1635. In this self-portrait Brouwer renders himself even more naturally, candidly and unselfconsciously. Here he is, just as he really was—unkempt, unshaven, without pretence. In this he would have had perfect freedom to portray himself as he felt, whereas Craesbeeck might well have been inhibited by a certain embarrassment. But in no wise does he appear to us here as the seedy vagabond that tradition would have him; far rather as a man who towards the end of his short life has raised himself beyond human vanity and equally beyond his obsession with human frailty and baseness. His late transition to landscape as a chief motif points in this direction, as also his search for the freedom and space to be found in nature which he approached so sensitively and rendered in so rarefied a manner and as something almost insubstantial. Thus this self-portrait is a very dignified document from the last period of the artist's brief span of life.

LIST OF WORKS DISCUSSED IN THE TEXT

N.B.: Numbers of reproductions to be found on the left-handside of the page. Roman numerals indicate colour plates.
'n.r.' means 'not reproduced'. The numbers of the pages refer to the text.

PART I

A. WORKS NOT BY BROUWER

31	Unidentified Painter, *Champion Drinker*, Rijksmuseum, Amsterdam; p. 56.
32	David Teniers, *Man with a Glass of Beer*, Musée du Louvre, Paris; p. 50.

B. COMPOSITIONS BY BROUWER, BUT NOT AUTOGRAPHIC

30	Copy after Brouwer, *Quartet*, City of York Art Gallery, York; pp. 57, 104.
33	— *Feast of the Cook*, studio repetition after Brouwer, possibly with his cooperation, Museum of Fine Arts, Boston; other copies: private collection Berlin (Bode 53), formerly collection S. von Schidlowski, Leningrad; pp. 57–59.
34	— *Tobacco Inn*, Dulwich College Picture Gallery; other copy: formerly Arenberg Collection (Bode 3); inferior copy Museum Valenciennes; pp. 59, 60, 114; a different and later copy of a part of this composition in the Prado, Madrid; pp. 59, 115; and a rough recast of the group on the left in the Lord Ellesmere Collection (Bridgewater Gallery); p. 61, footnote.

PART II

A. WORKS NOT BY BROUWER

35	Jan Lievens, *Portrait of Adriaen Brouwer*, collection F. Lugt, Paris; pp. 23, 48.
38	Frans Hals, *Merry Company*, Metropolitan Museum of Art, New York (Bequest of Benjamin Altman, 1913); pp. 11, 70.
53	Matthijs van den Bergh, *Peasants Dancing*, drawing after a painting by Brouwer, Ehem. Staatliche Museen, Berlin-Dahlem; pp. 92, 94.
120	Joos van Craesbeeck, *Portrait of Adriaen Brouwer*; present owner unknown; p. 182.

B. PAINTINGS BY BROUWER

I, 36	*Peasant's Feast*, Ruzicka Stiftung, Kunsthaus, Zürich; p. 65.
37	*Pancake Woman*, John G. Johnson Collection, Philadelphia, some doubts about authenticity; pp. 57, 70.
n.r.	*Pancake Woman*, Kunsthalle, Basel, same composition with small alterations, again doubts about authenticity; p. 57.
39	*Pancake Man*, John G. Johnson Collection, Philadelphia; pp. 57, 73.
40–43	*Fight over Cards*, Mauritshuis, The Hague (on loan from the Rijksmuseum); pp. 34, 78.
n.r.	*Tooth Puller*, (Bode 26); formerly Komter Collection; p. 81.
n.r.	*Peasants Dancing*, (Bode 23), formerly Schloss Collection, Paris, not up to standard; p. 82.
44	*Tavern Interior*, Museum Boymans-van Beuningen, Rotterdam; p. 84.
45	*Slaughter Feast*, Staatliches Museum, Schwerin; p. 84.
II	*Smokers*, Staatliche Kunstsammlungen, Kassel; p. 86.
III, 46–49	*Peasants Guzzling*, Mauritshuis, The Hague (on loan from the Rijksmuseum); p. 87.
IV	*The Moerdijk Peasants*, F. Markus Collection, Scarsdale (N.Y.); p. 89.

C. PAINTINGS AFTER BROUWER

D. WORKS BY UNIDENTIFIED PAINTERS WRONGLY ATTRIBUTED TO BROUWER

E. DRAWINGS BY BROUWER

F. DRAWINGS WRONGLY ATTRIBUTED TO BROUWER

TOPOGRAPHICAL LIST

VIENNA. Akademie der Bildenden Künste, *Landscape*, XIII, p. 167.

— Albertina, *Tavern Scene*, 69, p. 114.

— Albertina, *Two Cavaliers*, n.r. (see 75, 76), p. 120.

— Albertina, *Woman Spanking her Child*, n.r., p. 172.

— Czernin Collection, *Avaritia*, 99, p. 147.

WASSENAAR (Holland). Collection Louwman, *Organ Grinder*, 12, p. 34.

— Collection S. van den Bergh, *Peasants Dancing*, n.r., p. 36.

YORK. City of York Art Gallery, *Peasants Carousing* (Painter of the Large Jars), 2, pp. 32, 176.

— City of York Art Gallery, *Quartet*, 30, pp. 57, 104.

ZURICH. Kunsthaus, Ruzicka Stiftung, *Peasant's Feast*, I, 36, p. 65.

— Collection G. E. Bührle, *Village Scene*, 15, p. 36.

PRESENT OWNER UNKNOWN
f. means formerly

Smoker, (Painter of the Large Jars), 4, pp. 32, 177.

Small Landscape (Joos van Craesbeeck), 23, p. 42.

Man with a Great Cocked Hat, n.r., p. 152.

Portrait of Adriaen Brouwer (Joos van Craesbeeck), 120, p. 182.

f. Bayerische Staatsgemäldesammlungen, Munich, *Pigritia*, 98, p. 147.

f. Arenberg Collection, Brussels, *Tobacco Inn*, n.r. (see 34), pp. 59, 60, 114.

f. Collection M. van Gelder, Ukkel, Belgium and art dealer Katz, Dieren, Holland, *Three Men*, n.r., p. 92.

f. Goudstikker Collection, Amsterdam, *Man in a White Jacket*, n.r., p. 140.

f. Maurice Kann Collection, Paris, *Ira*, n.r., p. 147.

f. Collection Count Kersenbrock, Berlin-Grünewald, *Fight*, 9, p. 34.

f. Komter Collection, *Tooth Puller*, n.r., p. 81.

Collection von Pannwitz, f. Heemstede, *Four Children*, n.r., p. 159.

f. Collection S. von Schidlowski, Leningrad, *Feast of the Cook*, n.r. (see 33), pp. 57–59.

f. Schloss Collection, Paris, *Peasants Dancing*, n.r., p. 82.

f. Schloss Collection, Paris, *Messenger*, n.r., p. 111.

f. Schloss Collection, Paris, *Young Man with a Bulbous Nose*, n.r., p. 154.

f. Schloss Collection, Paris, *Laughing Young Man with a Beret and a Glass*, n.r., p. 154.

f. Stokvis Collection, Brussels, *Four Men Around a Table*, n.r., p. 145.

f. Art dealer Duits, London, *Young Man with Only a Couple of Teeth*, n.r., p. 153.

f. Art dealer Duveen, New York, *Ira*, n.r., p. 147.

f. Art dealer Goudstikker, Amsterdam, *Man with a Skull*, n.r., p. 150.

f. Art dealer Paul Graupe, New York, *Landscape with Five Men Playing at Ninepins*, n.r., p. 165.

Private Collection, f. Leonard Koetser, London, *Landscape* (Jan Lievens), 27, p. 49.

f. Art dealer D. Vaarties, Rotterdam, *Lame Musician*, 11, p. 35.

LITERATURE FREQUENTLY REFERRED TO IN THE TEXT

A. EARLY AUTHORS

Cornelis DE BIE: Gulden Cabinet van de edele vrij Schilder-Const, 1662.

Joachim VON SANDRART: Teutsche Academie, 1675.

Izaac BULLART: Académie des Sciences et des Arts, 1682.

Roger DE PILES: Abrégé de la Vie des Peintres, 1699.

Arnold HOUBRAKEN: Groote Schouburgh der Nederlantsche Konstschilders en Schilderessen, Amsterdam 1718.

B. LATER AUTHORS

Wilhelm SCHMIDT: Das Leben des Malers Adriaen Brouwer, Leipzig 1873.

F. Jos. VAN DEN BRANDEN: Adriaen de Brouwer en Joos van Craesbeeck. Nederl. Kunstbode III, Haarlem 1881.

Wilhelm BODE: Adriaen Brouwer, ein Bild seines Lebens und Schaffens. Die Grafische Künste VI 1884, 6, S. 21—72.

F. SCHMIDT DEGENER: Adriaen Brouwer, Brussel 1908.

C. HOFSTEDE DE GROOT: Beschreibendes und kritisches Verzeichnis der Werke der hervorragenden Holl. Maler d. 17. Jahrhunderts, III, 1910.

Wilh. VON BODE: Adriaen Brouwer, sein Leben und seine Werke, Berlin 1924.

Hans SCHNEIDER: Bildnisse A. Brouwers und seiner Freunde. Zeitschr. f. bild. Künste, 1926—27.

Hans SCHNEIDER: Bildnisse des Adriaen Brouwers. Festschrift f. M. J. Friedländer, Leipzig 1927.

Wilh. VON BODE: Kunsthist. Ausbeute aus der Deutschen Kunsthandel von heute. Rep. f. Kw. XLIX 1928.

E. J. REYNOLDS: Some Brouwer Problems, Lausanne 1931.

Hans SCHNEIDER: Jan Lievens, sein Leben und seine Werke, Haarlem 1932.

W. MARTIN: De Hollandsche Schilderkunst in de Zeventiende Eeuw, Vol. I, Amsterdam (n.d.)

Fr. WINKLER: Brouwers Raucher im Louvre, Pantheon XVII 1936.

Günter BÖHMER: Der Landschafter Adriaen Brouwer, München 1940.

Felix TIMMERMANS: Adriaen Brouwer (novel, 1946).

CONTENTS

PRINTED IN THE NETHERLANDS
BY JOH. ENSCHEDÉ EN ZONEN, HAARLEM